Australian Climate Policy and Diplomacy

Australian Climate Policy and Diplomacy provides a well overdue critique of existing, and high-profile, publications that convey the 'greenhouse mafia' hypothesis, which posits that Australia's weak policy response to climate change is the result of a menacing domestic fossil fuel lobby.

Ben L. Parr argues that the shared government–industry discourse about protecting Australia's industrial competitiveness has had a more decisive influence in shaping and legitimising Australian climate policy than the direct lobbying tactics of the fossil fuel industry. Parr also reveals how the divergent foreign policy discourses and traditions of Australia's two major political parties – as internationalist versus alliance-focused – have enabled and constrained their climate diplomacy and domestic policies over time. To demonstrate his argument, he presents a discourse analysis woven into a chronological policy narrative, comprising more than 1000 primary texts (media releases, interviews, and speeches) generated by prime ministers and key fossil fuel lobbyists. Overall, this volume illustrates how domestic forces have and are influencing Australia's climate policy. In doing so, it also provides a framework that can be adapted to examine climate mitigation policies in other countries, notably Canada and the US.

This book will be of interest to students and scholars of climate change, environmental policy and governance, and Australian climate change policy and politics more specifically, as well as policymakers and practitioners working in these fields.

Ben L. Parr holds a PhD in Political Science from the University of Melbourne, Australia, and has researched climate politics at the University of Melbourne for ten years.

Routledge Focus on Environment and Sustainability

Australian Climate Policy and Diplomacy

Government–Industry Discourses

Ben L. Parr

Routledge
Taylor & Francis Group

LONDON AND NEW YORK

First published 2020
by Routledge
2 Park Square, Milton Park, Abingdon, Oxon OX14 4RN

and by Routledge
52 Vanderbilt Avenue, New York, NY 10017

Routledge is an imprint of the Taylor & Francis Group, an informa business

First issued in paperback 2021

British Library Cataloguing-in-Publication Data
A catalogue record for this book is available from the British Library

Library of Congress Cataloging-in-Publication Data
Names: Parr, Ben L., author.
Title: Australian climate policy and diplomacy : government-industry discourses / Ben L. Parr.
Description: Abingdon, Oxon; New York, NY: Routledge, 2020. | Series: Routledge focus on environment and sustainability | Includes bibliographical references and index.
Identifiers: LCCN 2019043712 (print) | LCCN 2019043713 (ebook) | ISBN 9781138323827 (hardback) | ISBN 9780429451195 (ebook)
Subjects: LCSH: Climatic changes–Government policy–Australia. | Industrial policy–Australia. | Public-private sector cooperation–Australia.
Classification: LCC QC903.2.A8 P37 2020 (print) | LCC QC903.2.A8 (ebook) | DDC 363.738/745610994–dc23
LC record available at https://lccn.loc.gov/2019043712
LC ebook record available at https://lccn.loc.gov/2019043713

ISBN: 978-1-138-32382-7 (hbk)
ISBN: 978-1-03-208189-2 (pbk)
ISBN: 978-0-429-45119-5 (ebk)

Typeset in Times New Roman
by Wearset Ltd, Boldon, Tyne and Wear

Contents

Preface

Since the 1980s, scientists have reported that Australia is highly vulnerable to the physical impacts of global warming. Yet despite the warnings, successive Australian federal governments have failed to adopt strong greenhouse gas mitigation policies. The most common explanation for this lack of action has been the political influence of Australia's powerful mining industry over the policymaking processes and key decision-makers.

This book seeks to investigate this explanation by examining the relationship between the Australian federal government and the Australian fossil fuel mining lobby during the period 2010–2015, which covers the regression years on climate change policy between the Gillard Labor Government and the Abbott Coalition Government. The book critically examines Guy Pearse's and Clive Hamilton's popular 'greenhouse mafia' hypothesis, which argues that the lobbying tactics of the domestic fossil fuel lobby have largely determined Australian climate policy and, by implication, Australia's climate diplomacy.

The central argument of the book is that while the activities of the 'greenhouse mafia' have certainly been important in shaping Australia's failure to respond adequately to the climate challenge, it is the existence of a hegemonic discourse about industrial competitiveness (shared between governments of different political persuasions and industry actors) that has dominated the meaning of Australia's national interest, and shaped and constrained domestic climate policy and Australia's international negotiating positions. However, the differences in the major political parties' foreign policy discourses and identities – internationalist versus alliance-focused – have enabled and constrained Labor and Coalition governments in different ways, which helps to explain variation in climate diplomacy and domestic policy.

Acknowledgements

I would like to thank Routledge staff, Annabelle, Hannah, and Matthew, among others, for their professionalism, advice, and patience – it has been a great pleasure working with them. But most of all I would like to thank my family, Amelia and Luka, for putting up with my absence over many nights and weekends while researching and writing this book.

Introduction
Australian climate policy and politics

Australia is getting hotter. In 2017, the Australian continent sweltered through its third-warmest year on record (only 2005 and 2013 were warmer). In that year, the annual national mean temperature was 0.95 degrees Celsius above average. In 2018, this temperature measurement climbed to 1.14 degrees Celsius above average. January 2019 was Australia's hottest month on record (since 1910), with the country's mean temperature exceeding 30 degrees Celsius.[1] The Intergovernmental Panel on Climate Change (IPCC), the chief international body tasked with synthesising the science of climate change, has consistently reported that Australia is highly vulnerable to the physical impacts of climate change, including increasingly frequent heatwaves, bushfires, droughts, storms, and floods. The Commonwealth Scientific and Industrial Research Organisation (CSIRO), Australia's peak scientific research body, has repeatedly confirmed these findings. Yet despite the confluence of evidence and scientific warnings, successive Australian federal governments have failed to adopt strong greenhouse gas (GHG) mitigation policies. The present book investigates this puzzle.

The reluctance of Australian governments to take strong action on climate change can be traced back to the Hawke Labor Government's (1983–1991) adoption of a related to Interim Planning Target in October 1990. The target, which aimed to reduce carbon dioxide (CO_2) emissions by 20 per cent below 1988 levels by 2005,[2] came with a crucial caveat that environment minister, Graham Richardson (1987–1990 and 1994), announced to the Australian Senate in September 1991: 'The Government will not proceed with measures which have net adverse economic impacts nationally or on Australia's trade competitiveness in the absence of similar action by major greenhouse gas producing countries'.[3]

The release of the Keating Labor Government's (1991–1996) greenhouse policy in December 1992, the National Greenhouse Response Strategy, continued along this trajectory by only committing Australia

GHG emission mitigation polices that delivered net benefits, or at least no net economic costs, to Australian industry involved energy and minerals processing, production and use.[4] However, in the same year, environment minister, Ros Kelly (1991–1994 and 1995), signed, and would later help Australia ratify, the United Nations Framework Convention on Climate Change (UNFCCC), Article 3(1) of which included an obligation on the part of developed countries to lead in mitigation in accordance with the principle of common but differentiated responsibilities.

Elected in 1996, the Howard Liberal–National Coalition Government (1996–2007) consolidated Australia's preference for protecting the mining industry ahead of reducing GHG emissions. It did so most notably by playing an obstructionist role at the third Conference of the Parties (COP3) to the UNFCCC held in Kyoto during December 1997, by subsequently refusing to ratify the Kyoto Protocol, and by prioritising alliance-focused energy-based solutions to climate change such as uranium export deals and 'clean coal' partnerships.

The incoming Rudd Labor Government (2007–2010) ratified the Kyoto Protocol on 27 November 2007, three days after winning office, and set forth a path to establish a national emissions trading scheme (ETS) – the Carbon Pollution Reduction Scheme (CPRS). In an effort to protect Australia's fossil fuel sector, Rudd sought to link the CPRS to an expanded list of offsetting activities under the UNFCCC's 'flexibility mechanisms'. This policy was abandoned in April 2010.

The minority Gillard Labor Government (2010–2013) established the Clean Energy Act in November 2011, which would set a fixed price on carbon emissions in the period from July 2012 to July 2015 before moving into a fully-flexible ETS from July 2015. The Act comprised two principal functions that would help protect the competitiveness of Australia's fossil fuel industry: the Jobs and Competitiveness programme, and Energy Security Fund. Internationally, Australia signed up to the post-2012 period of the Kyoto Protocol at COP18 to the UNFCCC held in Doha during November and December 2012. This move committed Australia to a weak GHG emissions reduction target of 5 per cent below 2000 levels by 2020 (the CPRS target), but also ensured Australia's fossil fuel industry would be eligible to access cheap carbon offsets from developing countries. In June 2013, Kevin Rudd returned to the Prime Ministership. Two weeks later he announced that the ETS start date would commence in July 2014 (not 2015), reducing the liability on polluting industries by 75 per cent in 2015. He also again courted forest offsetting programmes abroad.

The Abbott Coalition Government (2013–2015) abolished the Gillard Government's carbon pricing mechanism in July 2014. It was replaced with 'Direct Action' measures, which included tree planting, energy efficiency measures, water recycling, and centrally, an Emissions Reduction Fund (ERF). The ERF, which as of November 2019 is still in operation (rebadged the Climate Solutions Fund), is a voluntary opt-in scheme that allocated $2.5 billion dollars of taxpayer funded subsidies to the fossil fuel industry to encourage them to reduce emissions. The Abbott Government did not send a minister to COP19 to the UNFCCC held in Warsaw in November 2013 (the first time since 1997); and at COP20 to the UNFCCC held in Lima in December 2014, Australia's Trade Minister, Andrew Robb, a reported climate sceptic, accompanied Australia's Foreign Minister, Julie Bishop, to avoid her committing Australia to a process or deal that may have negative consequences for Australia's big polluters and fossil fuel exporters. Abbott prioritised energy-based alliances similarly to Howard.

How can this series of policy outcomes be understood?

The two most comprehensive attempts to address this question are provided by Guy Pearse and Clive Hamilton.[5] Their mutually supportive analyses – Hamilton supervised Pearse's PhD thesis, from which Pearse's book arose – have come to dominate critical academic and popular understandings of why Australia's national climate policy has been overwhelmed by an enduring emphasis on protecting the mining and minerals industry. Indeed, their analyses constitute what might be called the 'interpretative orthodoxy'.

On 13 February 2006, the Australian Broadcasting Corporation's (ABC) flagship current affairs programme, Four Corners, aired a programme on Pearse's PhD thesis, written while he was a student at the Australian National University.[6] In the programme, Pearse revealed that he was granted full access to a small group of Canberra-based lobbyists who enthusiastically claimed, in a series of recorded interviews, that they had been manipulating Australia's greenhouse policy to protect Australia's large mining and minerals companies since the early 1990s. These lobbyists, the interviews revealed, called themselves the 'greenhouse mafia'. The 'greenhouse mafia' hypothesis, as portrayed by Four Corners, seemed to offer a highly plausible explanation as to why Australia had failed to establish strong GHG mitigation policies over time. In 2007, Pearse and Hamilton then released separate books, High and Dry, and Scorcher, respectively, which further popularised this conspiratorial understanding of Australian climate policy.

The present book aims to challenge the 'greenhouse mafia' hypothesis by offering a deeper explanation for Australia's weak response to the climate challenge. To achieve this, the book relocates responsibility for Australian climate policy and diplomacy away from Australia's domestic fossil fuel lobby, which has encountered widespread demonisation since

2006, and towards Australia's two major political parties – the Australian Labor Party, and the Liberal–National Coalition Party. Whereas the orthodox explanation has overwhelmingly focused on the Howard Government and its close links and networks with business and lobby groups, this book provides a critical analysis of the role of key traditions, values, ideas, and discourses that have shaped and constrained the ways in which both major parties have engaged with national and international climate policy. In other words, whereas the orthodox explanation has focused on some of the proximate causes of particular climate policy outcomes, this book directs attention to the underlying social elements that shape the field of possibilities.

The book argues that while the activities of the 'greenhouse mafia' have certainly been important in shaping Australia's failure to respond adequately to the climate challenge, a far more potent constraint is the existence of a deeply entrenched, background 'common-sense' discourse about industrial competitiveness (shared between governments of apparently different ideological persuasions and industry actors) that constructs the meaning of Australia's national interest on climate change, making some policies and international negotiating positions seem natural and necessary, while excluding others. Despite contestation over choice of policy instruments and differences in foreign policy traditions vis-à-vis multilateralism, the two parties share a deep-seated background consensus over industrial competitiveness that binds them together. This shared discourse on competitiveness has had a much more profound effect in shaping the boundaries and content of Australian climate policy than the role of specific veto players. Pearse's and Hamilton's analysis therefore, in my view, is incomplete because it neglects other, more potent but less visible dimensions of power – in this case the productive power of discourses.

Chapter outline

The book is divided into two Parts. Part I, comprising Chapters 1 and 2, presents an overview of the conceptual framework used to explain Australian climate policy and diplomacy in the period 2010–2015. The first chapter lays out the theoretical and methodological framework, while the second chapter provides a brief historical overview of the key discourses. The ultimate purpose of these chapters is to lay the groundwork for the analysis of the climate discourses that follows. Part II – Chapters 3 and 4 – present the findings of the discourse analysis of climate policy and diplomacy, which are woven into a chronological narrative of the key climate and energy policy outputs during the period from June 2010 to September

2015 – a period that encompasses the commencement of the Gillard Labor Government through to the end of the Abbott Coalition Government. The conclusion draws together the key findings of the book.

Notes

1 See, for example, *State of the Climate* reports (Bureau of Meteorology, 2017 and 2018), and 31 January 2019 announcement.
2 Harriet Bulkeley, 'The Formation of Australian Climate Change Policy: 1985–1995', in Alexander Gillespie and William C.G. Burns (eds), *Climate Change in the South Pacific: Impacts and Responses in Australia, New Zealand and the Small Island States* (Dordrecht: Kluwer, 2000), p. 37.
3 Graham Richardson, *Senate Hansard*, 4 September 1991. See also Clive Hamilton, *Running from the Storm: The Development of Climate Change Policy in Australia* (Sydney: UNSW Press, 2001), p. 33.
4 The National Greenhouse Response Strategy (Australian Government Publishing Services, 1992), p. 12.
5 Guy Pearse, *High and Dry: John Howard, Climate Change and the Selling of Australia's Future* (Camberwell, Victoria: Viking and the Penguin Group, 2007). Clive Hamilton, *Scorcher: The Dirty Politics of Climate Change* (Melbourne: Black Inc. Agenda, 2007).
6 Janine Cohen, 'The Greenhouse Mafia', Four Corners, ABC TV, 13 February 2006.

Part I
Conceptual framework

1 Theory and method

Renovating two-level games to explain Australian climate policy and diplomacy

An overview

As suggested in the Introduction, the book seeks to shift the focus away from the behaviour of industry lobbies with vested interests to political discourses. This shift exposes two key limitations in Pearse's and Hamilton's analysis about the influence of the 'greenhouse mafia'. First, their analysis concentrates primarily on domestic policy, to the relative neglect of international factors and foreign policy traditions. Second, the focus on political discourses in this book exposes Pearse's and Hamilton's rather simplistic, instrumental, theory of power, which is located in the hands of particular agents and exerted in the form of influence on policy outcomes according to standard Elite Theory. This is not to argue that this understanding of power is wrong (indeed both High and Dry, and Scorcher provide strong evidence to back their claims), but rather that it is incomplete because it neglects other, more potent but less visible dimensions of power – in this case the productive power of discourses, which can only be comprehended from a broader historical understanding of the evolution of policy discourses in the period preceding the development of climate policy.

To address the first limitation, I turn to Robert Putnam's 1988 theory of 'two-level games'.[1] Putman's two-level model provides a more expansive explanation in exploring how the political executive mediates between the domestic and international spheres, a process that he calls 'double-edged diplomacy'. Putnam's approach also focuses on the role of domestic veto coalitions in the context of domestic institutions, political parties, and elections, and seeks to show how these veto coalitions constrain the field of choice for the political executive in international negotiations – 'the win-set'. However, while the two-level model succeeds in addressing the first limitation in Pearse's and Hamilton's analysis by widening the lens of analysis, it also suffers from the second limitation. First, it is an interest-based theory that explains policy outcomes by privileging the power of domestic agents with vested interests in blocking or constraining diplomacy. Second, its theory of power is too reductive in understanding power simply as the ability of particular domestic agents to influence policy and diplomacy, based on the possession of material resources and institutional access. However, power is not simply something that is possessed by agents and 'applied' to block or influence particular policy outcomes; it can also be diffuse, indirect and inherent in social structures, including shared discourses, and operate in ways that reproduce particular understandings about what is possible and desirable and what is not.

This latter dimension of power has been acknowledged by other scholars of Australian climate policy, including in the work of Harriet Bulkeley (2000), Hayley Stevenson (2009), Peter Christoff (2005 and 2013), among others.[2] This body of scholarship is more relevant to this book because it examines the history of Australian climate policy discourses. Bulkeley's work, for example, identifies a network of domestic actors involved in what she calls Australia's 'resource-based discourse coalition' which, she suggests, can help us understand the continuity in Australian climate policy over time.[3] Likewise, Christoff's work shows that, despite the transition of government from Liberal to Labor, particular economic discourses have remained dominant, which accounts for Australia's weak policy responses to the urgent problem of climate change.[4] Stevenson's work identifies four elements – the national episteme, material resources, the political system, and institutional norms – that have helped shape Australian climate policy.[5] Although there is considerable variation in the approaches of these various authors, they all emphasise the role of discourses in maintaining policy continuity. Much has been written about institutional path dependency but this book seeks to highlight the lock-in effect of certain key discourses, or what might be called 'discursive path dependency'.

To shed further light on how discursive power, and its path dependency, works I introduce Antonio Gramsci's dual concepts of 'hegemony' and 'historic bloc' into Putnam's two-level model. This provides a more sophisticated understanding of 'win-sets' by allowing us to consider the 'veto role' of discourses. As suggested, this form of power is both productive and structural. That is, it 'produces' particular meanings and legitimates and enables certain policy options while also making other options unthinkable; and to the extent to which it is widely shared or saturated in the relevant political culture it operates as a social structure in constituting social roles (such as the role of government), relationships and ways of being in the world. This is important because in the empirical chapters I show that shared background discourses, and storylines, particularly about industrial competitiveness, which give rise to shared understandings of the meaning of national interests, can be even more potent in shaping Australian climate policy and diplomacy than the exercise of agential power through bribery and coercion of the kind emphasised in Guy Pearse's 'greenhouse mafia' thesis.

The theoretical and practical insights gleaned from this Gramscian renovation of the two-level model goes much further than the orthodox interpretation in explaining the puzzle raised in the beginning of the Introduction. However, these moves require asking a more precise research question that is able to determine empirically whether such a shared discourse exists between the government and fossil fuel industry groups and if so, how it has emerged and evolved, what are its characteristics, and whether and how it has shaped climate policy. The core research question under investigation in this book is therefore an empirical one that asks: *what is the relationship between government and industry climate change policy discourse from June 2010 to September 2015?*[6] This question is designed to direct attention to the crucial dimension of discursive power that is neglected in the work of Pearse and Hamilton.

Discourse analytic method

An overview

Discourse analysis is an ideal method to investigate the question above in a systematic fashion. Kristian Stokke explains that discourse analysis examines how discourses frame, characterise, legitimatise, and justify particular understandings and policies in ways that make them appear natural and necessary while excluding alternatives.[7] This book uses three discourse analytical categories – storylines, discourses, and discourse coalitions – previously deployed by Maarten Hajer (1995).[8] Hajer defines these terms in the following way. He explains that

> storylines are narratives on social reality through which elements from many different domains are combined and that provide actors with a set of symbolic references that suggest a common understanding ... essentially (they are a kind of narrative that) works as a metaphor.[9]

He defines discourse as 'an ensemble of ideas, concepts, and categories through which meaning is given to social and physical phenomena, and which is produced and reproduced through an identifiable set of practices'.[10] And he explains that 'a discourse coalition refers to a group of actors that, in the context of an identifiable set of practices, shares the usage of a particular set of storylines over a particular period of time'.[11] In term of their interaction. As we can see from these definitions, the articulation of a storyline simply cannot live up to the bulkiness of a discourse because unlike storylines, discourses contain values, worldviews, beliefs, ideologies, traditions, and storylines. Thus, we can understand storylines as constituting the more fine-grained regularities, alongside recurring tropes, metaphors etc. within the discursive structure. Thus, storylines represent only a subset of a discourse. Whereas a discourse coalition can be established if it can be shown that government ministers and industry lobbyists, for example, share the use of a set of storylines and/or discourses through a similar medium, such as speeches or media releases.

Ultimately, the book uncovers two key discourses on industrial competitiveness and foreign policy and show how they seek to fix the meaning of Australia's national interests on climate change. However, the advantage of deploying Hajer's analytical approach – as opposed to simply uncovering the key discourses – is that it illuminates the depth of government and industry compatibility, especially in storylines. Hajer's approach also makes it possible to identify not only the hegemonic discourse but also the key actors in the discourse coalition that makes up the relevant historic bloc in Gramsci's sense of the term. Finally, the analysis of discourses in the case study chapters is also punctuated with a series of Critical Discourse Moments, which are explained later.

I uncovered the key discourses and storylines that are characterised in Part II by examining and coding 1076 government and industry 'texts' (primarily media releases, interviews, and speeches) in the period from June 2010 to September 2015, made up of 767 'government texts', generated by Julia Gillard (499 texts), Kevin Rudd (16 texts) and Tony Abbott (252 texts) their respective minister responsible for climate change; and 309 'industry texts', generated by the Australian Coal Association (42 texts),[12] the Minerals Council of Australia (141 texts), and the Australian Petroleum Production and Exploration Association (126 texts). The Australian Coal Association acts on behalf of the black coal industry; the Minerals Council of Australia acts on behalf of the black coal and uranium industry;[13] and the Australian Petroleum Production and Exploration Association acts on behalf of the oil and gas/liquefied natural gas (LNG) industry. This discourse analysis is woven into a longitudinal climate (and energy) policy narrative, 2010–2015 (Chapters 3–4).

Case studies

The empirical chapters are Chapters 3 and 4. The study begins in June 2010 and concludes in September 2015. This period traverses the period of time commencing with the Gillard Labor Government (including Kevin Rudd's short return to the Prime Ministership in 2013) through to the conclusion of the Abbott Coalition Government. The purpose of this investigation is to uncover the extent to which political actors share similar storylines in order to determine whether they may be understood as forming part of a discourse coalition about industrial competitiveness. The chapters show that the industrial competitiveness discourse served as a 'master frame' in constructing the meaning of Australia's national interests on climate change, which has ultimately shaped Australian climate diplomacy and domestic policy for both major political parties and the fossil fuel industry between June 2010 and September 2015. This examination allows us to understand policy continuity over time. These chapters also reveal the existence of second key discourse about the foreign policy traditions of political parties. These divergent discourses allow us to understand change over time.

The following chapter outlines Australia's industrial competitiveness discourse and Australia's foreign policy discourses by way of an historical investigation.

Notes

1 Robert D. Putnam, 'Diplomacy and Domestic Politics: The Logic of Two-Level Games', *International Organization*, vol. 42, no. 3 (Summer 1988). See also, Peter B. Evans, Harold K. Jacobson, Robert D. Putnam, *Double-Edged Diplomacy: International Bargaining and Domestic Politics* (Berkeley: University of California Press, 1993).

2 See, for example, Robyn Eckersley, 'Poles Apart?: The Social Construction of Responsibility for Climate Change in Australia and Norway', *Australian Journal of Political and History*, vol. 59, no. 3 (2013), pp. 382–396. See also, Matt McDonald, 'Discourses of Climate Security', *Political Geography*, 33 (2013), pp. 42–51.

3 Harriet Bulkeley, 'Discourse Coalitions and the Australian Climate Change Policy Network', *Government and Policy*, vol. 18, 2000, pp. 727–748.

4 Peter Christoff, 'Climate Discourse Complexes, National Climate Regimes and Australian Climate Policy', *Australian Journal of Politics and History*, vol. 59, no. 3, 2013, pp. 349–367.

5 Hayley Stevenson, 'Cheating on Climate Change? Australia's Challenge to Global Warming Norms', *Australian Journal of International Affairs*, vol. 63, no. 2 (June 2009). pp. 165–186.

6 I use the term 'climate change policy' to refer to emission trading as well as energy-based solutions to climate change such as establishing domestic nuclear power programmes and uranium export deals, developing clean coal technology (i.e. Carbon Capture and Storage) and natural gas facilities and LNG

export deals. Essentially, policies that were deemed key components to the government's overall strategy to reduce emissions.

7   Kristian Stokke, 'The Soft Power of a Small State: Discursive Constructions and Institutional Practices of Norway's Peace Engagement', *Journal of Power, Conflict, and Democracy in South and Southeast Asia*, vol. 2, no. 1 (2010), p. 140.

8   Maarten Hajer, *The Politics of Environmental Discourse: Ecological Modernization and the Policy Process* (Oxford: Oxford University Press, 1995).

9   Hajer, *The Politics of Environmental Discourse*, pp. 62–63.

10 Hajer, *The Politics of Environmental Discourse*, p. 45.

11 Maarten Hajer, 'Coalitions, Practices, and Meaning in Environmental Politics: From Acid Raid to BSE', in David Howarth and Jacob Torfing (eds), *Discourse Theory in European Politics: Identity, Policy and Governance* (New York: Palgrave Macmillan, 2005), p. 302.

12 On 23 August 2013, the Australian Coal Association was dismantled and its corporate members were integrated into the Minerals Council of Australia.

13 The Minerals Council of Australia also represents other mined minerals including iron ore, gold, zinc, lead nickel, copper, bauxite, and alumina.

2 The key discourses

Introduction

Ultimately, Chapter 1 allows us to theorise about the existence of a 'veto discourse', rather than a simple 'veto player', à la, Guy Pearse's 'greenhouse mafia' thesis, over particular national climate policies and Australia's broader international negotiating position. Chapter 2 builds on this discussion by historicising the two key discourses relating to Australian climate policy and diplomacy, that is, the shared 'master discourse' about industrial competitiveness; and the divergent 'ancillary' foreign policy discourses of Australia's two major political parties – the Australian Labor Party and Liberal–National Coalition Party – as internationalist versus alliance-focused respectively. This discourse is characterised as 'ancillary' because despite their differences, both permit the executive to protect Australia's industrial competitiveness in Australian climate policymaking (as my discourse analysis chapters show), thus providing support to the 'master discourse'.

The first section of this chapter investigates Australia's industrial competitiveness discourse. The analysis commences in 1973, and not before, because this was a pivotal year in Australia's economic history where industrial reforms were justified purely on competitiveness grounds.[1] The latter section of the chapter deals with Australia's foreign policy discourses. This analysis commences in 1941 because it was only after the Second World War that Australia developed the desire and capacity to pursue its foreign policies independently of Britain.

Understanding continuity

Australia's industrial competitiveness discourse

Australia's industrial competitiveness discourse has four key phases. The first phase began in 1973 and ended in 1987. In this period of time the idea of competitiveness evolved. It began as a rhetorical device wielded by the Whitlam Labor Government, predominantly Labor Right faction (which included Whitlam), and was continued by the Fraser Liberal Government, to justify tariff cuts and the reduction of government support for selected industries. The incoming Hawke Labor Government of 1983 built on this agenda, further retreating from Labor's founding economic discourse about protectionism. Hawke's reforms were broadly supported by the Labor Right (which included Hawke), the Liberal Party (minus the Country Party component), Canberra's economic bureaucracies (i.e. Treasury), and the export orientated mining sector. To varying degrees this coalition of actors argued for lower tariffs and a hands-off approach to industry. The opposing coalition consisted of the Labor Left and some manufacturing unions. This group argued that government must maintain tariff walls and continue to support selected struggling industries to protect jobs and prosperity. During this period, Australia's key allies, the United Kingdom and the United States, were also reforming their economies to make domestic industry more efficient, productive, and ultimately, internationally competitive. By 1987 competitiveness-based reforms (that is, governments intervening in the marketplace to foster company rivalry) had gained strong support from across the political spectrum.

The second phase began in 1988 and ended in 1996. By 1988, the idea of industrial competitiveness had become a fully-fledged and established discourse that incorporated its own values, worldviews and beliefs. This discourse served to structure Labor's field of decision making, which made the continuation of competitive-based reforms seem natural and necessary. In 1988 and 1991, the Hawke Government undertook two rounds of tariff reductions. These reforms made the effective rate of protection on industry almost negligible, all-but demolishing Labor's protectionist tradition. However, Hawke's 'positive interventionist' approach to industry still courted Labor's earlier hands-on approach from the 1970s. By 1991, pursuing reforms that enhanced domestic rivalry between firms had become a common-sense view held by both major political parties and Canberra's economic elites. The consensus view was that continuing to roll-back tariffs and workplace protections would make industry more efficient and productive, which would ultimately benefit the nation and Australian society. In 1991 the incoming Keating Labor Government pursued competitive-based reforms with considerable vigour. In comparison to his predecessor, Keating stressed the 'public interest' dimension of competitive-based reforms. This aspect would inform the 1993 Hilmer Review on national competition policy, and ultimately, the 1995 establishment of the Australian Consumer and Competition Council (ACCC). Under Keating, the competitiveness discourse spilled over from the economic and political sphere to begin to rule the general conduct of social life in Australia.

The third phase began in 1997 and ended in 2008. The incoming conservative Howard Government pushed the industrial competitiveness discourse to its extreme by introducing radical workplace relations reforms and establishing multiple Free Trade Agreements (FTAs). The Howard Government used Labor's reforms as a springboard for these competitive-based reforms. Australia's fossil fuel mining industry continued to benefit greatly, while manufacturing suffered. The Howard Government won four consecutive elections holding office from 1996 to 2007, which is a testimony to public acceptance of the competitiveness ideology. The election victory of the Labor Party under Kevin Rudd in 2007 tamed Howard's extreme competitive-based policies. Rudd reinstituted 'fairer' workplace relations and worked through multilateral forums rather than through bilateral agreements to liberalise the global economy. Despite these moderations, and proclaiming that market fundamentalism was 'dead' in the wake of the 2008 Global Financial Crisis (GFC), Rudd's policies still reinforced the competitiveness hegemony. The naturalisation of this discourse is problematic for Social Democratic governments because there is a strong incentive to repeal 'fairer' economic policies in search of competitiveness gains.

The fourth phase commenced in 2009 and continues to the present day. Emerging out of the 2008 GFC, Australia's political leaders doubled down on the nation's competitiveness agenda. Gillard held the line on competitiveness in the workplace, but intensified it in education; and supported free trade via FTAs or multilateralism. Rudd, during his fleeting return to the Prime Ministership in 2013, announced a 'new competitiveness agenda' designed to intensify competition in the non-resource sectors. Abbott – who was ideologically opposed (almost suspicious) of government involvement in social or economic relations – rolled back a raft of 'anti-competitiveness' regulations on the fossil fuel sector, established FTA's with Australia's major fossil fuel export destinations, and reregulated to extend and strengthen the hand of competitiveness in Australia's social sectors, healthcare and education for example, via the recommendation of the 2015 Harper Review – the most comprehensive review of competition since the Hilmar Review.

Overlaying the above discussion, which has focused primarily on workplace relations reforms, and tariffs and trade, successive Australian governments of both political persuasions have also sought to boost the competitive position of the Australian fossil fuel sector compared to other countries by privatising, and investing directly in, mining infrastructure and offering generous subsidy packages. For example, the Hilmer Review supported Keating's infrastructure privatisation agenda, arguing that greater international competitiveness could be achieved by privatising major infrastructure and transport corridors such as rail and ports – both critical pieces of infrastructure for the export orientated mining industry. Numerous privatisations followed. More than two decades later Australian governments are still committed to proposing competitive-based incentives to attract global mining capital. For example, Australian governments of both major political persuasions had considered offering the Adani Group, a global mining company based in India, A$1 billion dollars to construct a rail line to transport coal for export.

The next section examines Australia's foreign policy discourses.

Understanding change

Australia's foreign policy discourses

For most of the twentieth century, geopolitics and security concerns drove Australian foreign policy. Australia felt isolated in a hostile part of the world, which was confirmed by Australia's near invasion by the Japanese forces in 1942, and later, the perceived threat of Chinese-based communism and the Vietnam War in the 1960s and 1970s. For the Curtin and Chifley Labor Governments (1941–1949), Australia's first post-war governments, Australia's security interests would be best served by shaping the UN's processes to maximise the influence of smaller and middle powers such as Australia, while diluting the influence of more powerful states. The Menzies Liberal Government (1949–1966) was similarly preoccupied with security concerns. But unlike Labor, for post-war Liberal's Australia's security interests would be protected by maintaining strong relations with Britain and America – as Menzies would famously declare, Australia will find security through its 'great and powerful friends' (not via the UN).

In the aftermath of the Vietnam War, the Whitlam Labor Government's (1972–1975) core interest in foreign affairs was to distance Australia from the US, which it did by prioritising the UN and regularly voting against the US in the United Nations General Assembly (UNGA). Whitlam himself also sought to diminish Australia's sense of isolation within its own region. He wanted Australians to understand that Asia was an opportunity, not something to fear – which commenced Australia's 'turn to Asia'. The Hawke and Keating Governments showed a strong commitment to UN processes and protocols to advance Australia's interests, and added considerably to Labor's traditions, most notably with the advent of 'good international citizen'. Australia's 'turn to Asia' was elevated to astronomic levels at the end of the Cold War in 1989 under Hawke and Keating who realised that Australia had a lot to gain, in terms of both protecting and advancing Australia's economic and security interests, by fuelling Asia's industrialisation with its natural resources. But for Australia to compete in this increasingly globalised world post-Whitlam, it had to modernise its domestic economy to make it more efficient (which was the subject of the above section).

The Howard Coalition Government (1996–2007) released Australia's first ever White Paper on foreign and trade policy. It explicitly prioritised bilateralism over multilateralism, particularly via the UN, as a means of advancing Australia's interests. Australia's interests and identity under Howard was as a core part of the Anglo-American alliance, but with a strong commercial tie to Asia. The Rudd Labor Government's (2007–2010) foreign policy discourse provided strong continuity with Labor predecessors, particularly in terms of seeking to shape multilateral processes to serve Australia's economic, security, and environmental interests (e.g. centralising the G20 as the premier financial forum for world leaders to discuss responses to the Global Financial Crisis, replacing the G8, seeking a non-permanent seat on the UN Security Council in 2013–2014 and ratifying the Kyoto Protocol). However, similarly to Howard, the Rudd Labor Government also saw China, and some other parts of Asia, as potentially threatening, which led to a strong commitment to the US alliance, while it also deepened Australia's commercial ties with the region, and particularly China.

Prime Minister Julia Gillard's foreign policy discourse remained consistent with Labor traditions. Under Gillard, 'Australia was a strong supporter of the UN', evoking Labor's internationalist tradition.[2] But she was less enthusiastic about working via multilateral channels compared to Rudd. Rather, she saw her talents as building close bilateral relations. She would also express the Labor ideas of activism and good international citizenship, including on climate change.[3] Gillard described Australia as a 'confident middle power', the prefix serving to signal to Asia that Australia was prepared for what she described as 'The Asian Century'. Indeed, her 2012 White Paper of the same name would be Gillard's central contribution to Australia's foreign policy. Gillard's engagement with Asia prioritised economic matters – particularly energy and mineral resources, coal, LNG (and uranium with India) which are of 'shared interest' and 'mutual benefit', she explained – but with a distinct flavour of engagement beyond commercial interests, something that was largely absent under Rudd and Howard; yet she did not take this socio-cultural affinity as far as Keating. But she also hedged her bets. Gillard was unreservedly enthusiastic about the closeness or 'mateship', shared values and history that underpinned the US–Australia relationship, which accompanied a personal fondness towards President Barack Obama not seen since that between John Howard and George W. Bush.

Prime Minister Tony Abbott's foreign policy discourse exhibited realism, bilateralism, Anglo-sphere relations, and regionalism – all expressed in a more aggressive style than Howard. Abbott believed that Australia had a strong values-based connection to Britain and the Commonwealth, as well as Canada under Conservative Prime Minister, Stephen Harper. Such was Abbott's veneration of Britain and the Monarchy, described as his 'blind spot', that it contributed to his demise as Prime Minister after awarding a knighthood to the Queen's husband, Prince Philip precipitated nation-wide ridicule. He was a strong supporter of US alliance, however, his awkward relationship with the progressive Obama Administration suggests that he prioritised a personal values-based alignment over a national interest alignment. Under Abbott, what counted in Australia's foreign relations was what could be called a 'values-sphere'. Abbott showed distain for the UN itself, its processes and protocols, particularly as they related to climate change and refugees. He operationalised this distain under the mantra: 'we want more Jakarta, and less Geneva' in our foreign policy.[4] Yet, despite this apparent Jakarta focus, Abbott's boat push-back (asylum seeker) policy soured relations with Indonesia considerably. He would only seek a commercial/transactional relationship with Asia more broadly. Abbott came to the top job renowned for his disinterest in foreign policy and showed limited imagination in the portfolio as Prime Minister – as did his Foreign Minister, Julie Bishop.

Conclusion

The first section of this chapter showed that in the period of time between 1973 and 2015 Australian governments of both political persuasions were pursuing very similar economic agendas. Improving the international competitiveness of Australia's big fossil fuel mining companies, and through them, the economy in general, was a bipartisan nation building agenda. The fossil fuel lobby's contemporary disproportionate presence in Australian politics was predominantly due to the sector they represent being identified as the driving force behind delivering a more competitive and prosperous Australia. In this sense, Australia's fossil fuel sector was the focus of a transformational government agenda, not some external agitator manipulating government process to secure reforms, including on climate change, in their interests as Guy Pearse's 'greenhouse mafia' thesis suggests. Indeed, the issue of global warming only began to appear on international policymaker's radar in the late 1980s, mid-way through Australia's industrial competitiveness agenda.

The case study (discourse analysis) chapters to follow show that the industrial competitiveness discourse dominated the meaning of Australia's national interest on climate change, which structured the field of government and industry decision making, which served to veto certain national climate policies and broader international negotiation positions. Revealing this deeply entrenched discourse about competitiveness helps us to understand the continuity in Australian climate policy from 2010 to 2015, and provides novel insights to this book's overall puzzle that seeks to address Australia's vulnerability-action mismatch.

The second section of this chapter historicised Australia's divergent foreign policy discourses from 1941 to 2015. It showed that Labor governments sought to shape UN processes to protect Australia's interests, whereas the Liberal governments sought to build alliances and interest-based coalitions to the same end. These findings are important for the case study chapters because they show that Coalition governments protected Australia's interests in resource mining by cultivating energy-based partnerships and loose coalitions (i.e. uranium exporting partnerships) as solutions to climate change; whereas Labor governments sought to shape the UNFCCC processes to the same end. However, critically, Australia's alternative foreign policy discourses (and identities) also put more and less pressure on each party to pursue strong GHG mitigation policies. This insight helps us understand variation in Australian climate policy and diplomacy over time.

Overall, Part I suggests that the convergent and divergent economic and foreign policy discourses of Australia's two major political parties, set within the historical context of war and peace in 1945, 1973, and 1989, is a much better starting point from which to explore Australian climate policy and diplomacy than the relatively shallow 'greenhouse mafia' thesis. However, the analysis is not necessarily at odds with this thesis since these actors were at the forefront of supporting the competitiveness agenda.

Part II shows that the economic and foreign policy discourses of Australia's two major political parties can account for continuity and change in Australian climate change policy and diplomacy from June 2010 to September 2015.

Notes

1 Eric Hobsbawn identifies 1973 as the beginning of 'market fundamentalism' and ponders whether the Global Financial Crisis (GFC) in 2008 signalled its end. See also, 'The Rudd Essay & the GFC' (responses), *The Monthly*, no. 45 (May 2009) www.themonthly.com.au (Accessed 04/02/2013).

2 Julia Gillard, 'Making a Difference for the Small and Medium Countries of the World', Speech to the African Union Permanent Representatives, New York, 10 March 2011.

3 Julia Gillard, 'Making a Difference for the Small and Medium Countries of the World', Speech to the African Union Permanent Representatives, New York, 10 March 2011.

4 Tony Abbott, 'Remarks at Sydney Airport', 30 September 2013. See also Tony Abbott: 'Address to Western Australian Liberal Party State Council', 9 November 2013; 'Press Conference', Sydney, 15 December 2013; 'Address to The Parliamentary Reception for Their Royal Highnesses the Duke and Duchess of Cambridge', 24 April 2014; 'Address to the 57th Liberal Party Federal Council', 28 June 2014.

Part II

The cases

Background

In the evening of 23 June 2010, Julia Gillard, the Deputy Prime Minister of Australia, requested that incumbent Prime Minister of Australia since 2007, Kevin Rudd, hold a leadership ballot to determine the leadership of the Australian Labor Party and, by implication, the Prime Ministership. Kevin Rudd agreed and called for a special meeting to be held the following day at 9:00 am for the vote.

The following morning, Julia Gillard won the leadership ballot unopposed. Kevin Rudd did not contest, choosing to instead resign. At midday, Kevin Rudd, still as Prime Minister – but no longer Labor leader – delivered an emotional speech outlining his government's achievements (and failures). Among them was climate change:

> I'm proud of the fact that the first thing we did in government was ratify the Kyoto Protocol. I'm proud of the fact that we boosted the renewable energy target to 20%. I'm proud of the fact that we tried three times to get emissions trading through this Parliament. Although we failed. And if I'd add one point on future policy. It must be our ambition to pass a carbon pollution reduction scheme within this parliament – the one that follows I mean. So we can make a difference, a real difference, to climate change.[1]

That afternoon, Julia Gillard was sworn-in as the 27th Prime Minister of Australia and first female Prime Minister. Rudd was gone. For now.

Note

1 Kevin Rudd, 'Final Press Conference as Prime Minister', Canberra, 24 June 2010.

3   The Gillard Labor Government (including Rudd 2013)

Introduction

Chapter 3 explores Australian climate policy and diplomacy during the Gillard Labor Government, which commenced in June 2010 and concluded in June 2013; and during the short return of the Rudd Labor Government, from June 2013 to September 2013 (the Labor Party, led by Kevin Rudd, were also in office during the period 2007–2010).

This chapter reveals the key discourses that shaped and legitimated climate policy and diplomacy for the Gillard Government and the Australian fossil fuel lobby – the Australian Coal Association (ACA), the Minerals Council of Australia (MCA) and Australian Petroleum Production and Exploration Association (APPEA). It shows that key government actors – principally Prime Minister Julia Gillard, but also climate minister, Greg Combet, and key fossil fuel lobbyists, principally, chief officers Ralph Hillman, then John Pegler and Nikki Williams (ACA), Mitch Hooke (MCA) and Belinda Robinson, then David Byers (APPEA) – shared a 'master discourse' about industrial competitiveness, which dominated the meaning of Australia's national interest, and served to make some (weaker) climate policies and negotiating positions possible, while excluding (stronger) others. In this sense, Chapter 3 shows, metaphorically speaking, the silent veto role of a domestic discourse. This insight presents a deeper alternative compared to Pearse's (and Putnam's) simple agential greenhouse mafia thesis. This shared background consensus about competitiveness provides evidence of what Gramsci terms an 'historic bloc'.

This chapter also reveals the existence of an 'ancillary discourse' about Labor's foreign policy traditions. This discourse legitimated the Gillard Government's diplomatic focus on climate multilateralism and tied her Government to the obligations of the UNFCCC, which required a commitment to stronger domestic climate policies. We see that while Labor's internationalist discourse conflicted with the competitiveness discourse, it also permitted scope for Gillard to shape the UNFCCC process to serve Australia's economic interests. This chapter also investigates the role that storylines play in shaping and justifying policies. It explores the role of the two storyline binaries that are conceptually positioned underneath the 'master discourse': the cost-to-act (CTA) versus the cost-not-to-act (CNTA) storylines; and the lose–lose (LL) versus the win–win (WW) storylines.

The first storyline binary served to frame the establishment of a national carbon pricing mechanism (CPM). By way of background, Prime Minister John Howard deployed the CTA storyline throughout his Prime Ministership to delegitimise the establishment of a national CPM. Howard's view was that a CPM would compromise industrial competitiveness and therefore 'cost' jobs, investment, and government revenue. However, in the period 2006–2007, a range of actors (i.e. The Stern Report of 2006, and Prime Minister Rudd in 2007) deployed the opposing CNTA storyline, which posits that delaying the establishment of a CPM would only serve to increase the social and environmental 'costs' over time and thereby encourages governments to act immediately to reduce GHG emissions. This advocacy served to challenge the CTA storyline for dominance, and eventually replace it in the latter part of 2007. Prime Minister Kevin Rudd consolidated the dominant position of the CNTA storyline by routinely deploying it to justify the establishment a nation-wide emissions trading scheme – the now fated Carbon Pollution Reduction Scheme.

As we shall see, throughout 2010 and 2011, five Critical Discourse Moments, which can be defined as moments 'marked by particular events that potentially challenge existing discursive positions and constructs or, in contrast, may contribute to their further sedimentation',[1] are identified where Prime Minister Gillard weakened the CNTA storyline, and in doing so, allowed the CTA storyline to re-emerge, wielded to great effect by opposition leader Tony Abbott, as the dominant storyline to frame Australian climate policy.

The second set of storylines WW, LL are deployed by government and industry to either legitimise a suite of CPM policy settings (i.e. the allocation of free permits) or justify particular energy-based solution (i.e. LNG exports). The WW storyline simply means that a particular policy, or suite of measures, is good for the environment (i.e. will reduce global emissions) and is good for the economy (i.e. protects jobs, investment, and government revenue). The LL storyline simply states the opposite. This chapter shows that both government and industry regularly deployed the WW, LL storyline to justify certain carbon pricing design features, so it wasn't simply about opposing the scheme for the fossil fuel lobby, is was about shaping it; as well as to justify energy-based solutions. The story begins on 24 June 2010.

* * *

At 2:30 pm on 24 June 2010, Prime Minister Julia Gillard rose in the Australian Federal Parliament for *Question Time* and said: 'This morning I was elected as leader of the parliamentary Labor Party. I accept that the Government has lost track. We will get back on track. I have taken control for precisely this purpose'.[2] Outraged – despite a similarly method of ascendency in December 2009 – opposition leader Tony Abbott retorted: 'A midnight knock on the door followed by political execution is no way that the Australian Prime Minister should be treated'.[3]

Kevin Rudd had championed Australia's first serious attempt to establish a national emissions trading scheme – the Carbon Pollution Reduction Scheme (CPRS), albeit with design elements that delivered significant concessions to Australia's high emitting industries. Yet, in coming to power, Gillard would demote carbon pricing as a priority policy response to climate change. While Gillard did confirm that a national price on carbon was required 'in the future', she would not be drawn on the precise mechanism, she declined to take the CPRS to a double dissolution election (despite the trigger being available), she would not accept the separate proposals put forward by the Australian Greens Party and prominent climate economist Ross Garnaut for a two-year interim carbon tax to be adopted, and she argued that any future price on carbon would be dependent on satisfying a series of prerequisites, namely, only *if* 'global economic conditions improve', 'our economy strengthens', and most importantly, a domestic 'community consensus' in support of a carbon pricing could be achieved.[4] In the meantime, Gillard explained, the government would pursue 'practical measures' such as building low pollution and renewable electricity infrastructure.

This reprioritisation of climate policies was accompanied by a stark change in language. For Rudd, climate change represented 'the great moral challenge of a generation', and a threat to 'our kids', national security and the planet – all of which signalled that the cost of delay far exceeds the costs of immediate action to reduce emissions. For Gillard, by contrast, as she explained on her first day as Prime Minister: 'I believe in climate change … (and) I believe that human beings contribute to it'.[5] Thus, unlike Rudd, Gillard did not deploy the CNTA storyline to frame her Government's policy response to climate change, which left Tony Abbott's CTA unchallenged. The absence of the CNTA storyline at this highly visible political event – replacing a sitting Prime Minister – was a major missed opportunity; and therefore, can be considered the first Critical Discourse Moment in the Gillard years. It would commence the return of the CTA storyline to a position of dominance, having been subordinated for the period of the Rudd Government (November 2007–June 2010) by the CNTA storyline.[6]

By early July however, it was becoming apparent that Labor was losing voters to the Australian Green Party. Labor voters had serious misgivings about Gillard's pathway to the top job, one that sidelined the electorate. To sure-up her prospects in the Federal Election, which she had previously announced would take place on 21 August 2010, Labor struck a preference deal with the Greens. A suite of climate change policies followed. These included, most prominently, if re-elected, a commitment to establish a 'Citizen Assembly' charged with forging a 'community consensus' in support of establishing a price on carbon after 2012 and investigating the consequences of such a scheme. In the interim period, between 2010 and 2012, a future Gillard Government would introduce policies to discourage the construction of new high-polluting coal fired power stations, reward businesses for reducing emissions, and invest in renewables, among other things.[7]

To justify these policies, Gillard deployed the environmentally focused CNTA storyline for the first time as Prime Minister, which she repeatedly operationalised at an international and national level of abstraction. For example, 'the consequences of inaction are ultimately threatening for our planet', and 'the price of inaction is too high a price for our country to pay'.[8] She would also deploy the WW storyline to justify the government's climate policies identified above (i.e. these policies are good for the economy and good for the environment).

In early August the polls had closed significantly, indicating a 50/50 split between Labor and the Coalition. In response, the Prime Minister promised to unleash 'the real Julia', unfettered by 'stage-managed events' that she believed were stifling her natural flare and style.[9] This announcement precipitated a media frenzy on what constituted the 'real' and 'fake' Julia, significantly reducing Gillard's media time for policy discussion. Kevin Rudd was also reportedly leaking again Gillard, for instance that she had opposed pension increases and paid parental leave as his Deputy.[10] In addition, the 'Citizen Assembly' idea was being ridiculed by the political right and left – the former argued that the Parliament was the place to debate this issue, while the latter argued that given 2009 was Australia's hottest year on record there was no time to lose. Both agreed that it showed a lack of leadership. Additional criticism was lumped on the Prime Minister for apparently failing to consult with the Cabinet on the Assembly idea. This charge was particularly problematic for Gillard because she had removed Kevin Rudd in part based on his propensity to make decisions without consulting Cabinet colleagues.[11] In response, Gillard argued that establishing a community consensus was essential because legislating a carbon price clearly required a more robust consensus than the thin political consensus negotiated by her predecessor in the Parliament.

In this milieu of intrigue and innuendo, little space was left for policy discussion of any kind. Beyond responding to criticisms about the Assembly, Gillard would mostly draw basic distinctions between her position on climate change and her opponent, Tony Abbott. For example, I believe in the science of climate change, he is sceptical; I want to make big polluters pay, he wants to pay polluters; I want to price carbon, he doesn't.[12]

On 16 August, just five days before the Federal Election, Labor launched its election campaign – the shortest election campaign in Australian political history. In her speech, Gillard devoted one line to climate change, a rather uninspiring: 'we will work together and tackle climate change'.[13] And as if things could not get any worse, in an interview that evening, the Prime Minister delivered a remark that would haunt her for the remainder of her time in the Parliament: 'There will be no carbon tax under the government I lead'.[14]

By the morning of 20 August 2010, election eve, the Prime Minister's primary vote had slumped to just 35 per cent – the same as Rudd's when Gillard removed him. Later in the day, in her final interview before polling, Gillard conceded that a price on carbon would not be legislated until after the next election in three more years, if Labor were to win – which would constitute federal Labor's third election mandate to price carbon (Rudd in November 2007, Gillard tomorrow in 2010, and a future Labor win in 2013).[15] This was troublesome, particularly for progressive voters, because it lent further support to a sense that Gillard was not really committed to carbon pricing.

The results of the Australian Federal Election of 21 August 2010, delivered, as expected, a minority government to the Labor Party and reinstated Julia Gillard as Prime Minister. But this wasn't without drama.

Labor and the Coalition both won 72 seats in the 150-seat House of Representatives (Lower House), which was four shy of the required 76 seats to form a majority government. This predicament, which resulted in the first hung parliament since the election of 1940, triggered a period of furious backroom negotiating by the major parities with the six crossbenches that held the balance of power, comprising one Green and five Independents. Eventually, four of the six crossbenches declared their support for Labor, delivering Gillard the 76 seats she needed to form a minority government. Abbott and the Coalition were left with 74 seats. But the real drama was in the Senate. In the 76-seat Senate (Upper House) Labor had only won 31 seats and the Coalition 34 seats. Critically, the Greens had won sole balance of power with nine senators elected. On 1 September, Gillard signed an Agreement with the Greens (and Independents) – covering all Greens parliamentarians. The so-called 'Labor–Greens Agreement', would, on the one hand, secure the support of the Greens in the Lower and Upper houses, and ultimately allow Gillard to form government, and on the other hand, the Agreement stipulated that Gillard must establish a committee of parliamentarians who were committed to establishing a price on carbon pollution (with the overarching goal to legislate the price in this term of government). And it was on *this* basis that on 7 September 2010, the Gillard Minority Government was announced.

A few days later, on 11 September, Gillard announced her new Cabinet. The former Prime Minister Kevin Rudd would become Foreign Minister – removing his material presence from the Cabinet for large chunks of the year. Penny Wong, climate minister since 2007, would be moved to finance. Martin Ferguson would continue in the resource and energy portfolio. And Greg Combet, the highly experienced trade union campaigner and negotiator, would be elevated to the Cabinet as minister for climate change.[16]

Australia's coal and gas/LNG lobbies cautiously welcomed the new government, clearly concerned about the influence that the Greens may exert over policy, particularly on climate change.[17] In response to the election result, both the ACA and the APPEA deployed the WW storyline to help legitimise the energy-producing operations of their corporate members, and in doing so, hopefully garner concessions from the newly formed federal government. The ACA's Chief, Ralph Hillman, argued that 'Carbon capture and storage (CCS) will be essential to reduce Australian and global emissions while maintaining energy security', and therefore, a continued financial commitment from the government to its development was needed.[18] The APPEA's Chief, Belinda Robinson, argued that Australia's gas industry has the potential to 'underpin a strong and stable economy, provide energy security for households and industry, and assist in the transition to a less carbon intensive future', and therefore, clarity on carbon pricing was needed to ensure that it encouraged gas/LNG expansion, not constrain it.[19]

Hillman too was concerned about a future carbon price. He was more specific than Robinson in his request, arguing that fugitive emissions from coal mines must be deemed eligible for compensation under any future carbon pricing scheme, failure to do so, he warned 'would have a major impact on the international competitiveness of the coal industry – Australia's largest export industry – and ultimately cost jobs'.[20] The MCA's Chief, Mitch Hooke, curtly welcomed the incoming government in the following way: the Australian government, 'the Australian minerals industry and all Australians' have a shared interest in protecting the 'international competitiveness' of the coal industry.[21]

As the government settled in, speculation in the media heightened about the Prime Minister's intentions to establish a carbon price. Gillard would not rule-in or out a fixed price on carbon. I would prefer a market mechanism, she repeatedly affirmed, 'but we've agreed with the Greens that we have an inclusive climate change committee to work through the options'.[22] Based on this justifiable tentativeness, Abbott immediate claimed that 'Yesterday, Labor said that maybe there would be a carbon tax after all'.[23]

On 27 September 2010, the Prime Minister announced that the government had established a Multi-Party Committee on Climate Change (MPCCC), open to parliamentarians from all sides of politics who 'agree that climate change is real and that we need to price carbon'.[24] Ultimately, the MPCCC would comprise the Prime Minister, Treasurer Wayne Swan, and Minister Combet from the government; the Greens Party leader, Bob Brown and his Deputy Christine Milne; and Independent, Tony Windsor. Abbott and the Coalition declined any involvement. The MPCCC's task was to 'work through the options' to price carbon pollution. At the announcement, Gillard did not deploy an environmentally focused CNTA storyline to frame the MPCCC's policy work. Rather, she (and Combet) deployed an economic interpretation of the CNTA storyline, operationalised at an international level: 'if we fail to act on a price on carbon pollution we, of course, run a risk of falling behind globally'.[25] The Prime Minister also asserted that a price on carbon was in Australia's national interests.

Later in the week, Gillard would repeatedly deploy the economic CNTA storyline, this time operationalised at a local level, to justify the establishment of a nation-wide carbon price (i.e. a price on carbon will incentivise investment in electricity generation and avoid power price rises. By contrast, inaction means business won't invest in long-lived assets which will mean higher power prices).[26] The absence of the environmental CNTA storyline at the MPCCC announcement – the most important announcement to date on climate change – is good reason to identify this event, and its immediate aftermath, as the second Critical Discourse Moment in the Gillard years.

The following day, 28 September 2010, the Rudd Government's CPRS legislation lapsed in the Senate.

In October, Gillard's domestic climate and energy agenda was full. On 7 October, the MPCCC held its first meeting at which members agreed to

drop the much-maligned 'Citizens Assembly' idea – leaving public aware-
ness to the newly created Climate Change Commission and other government and expert outreach. The following day, Gillard released the Prime
Minister's Task Group on Energy Efficiency report: energy efficiency is a
key component to tackling climate change, she declared.[27] The next day, 9
October, she flew to Chevron's 'Gorgon' project off the Western Australia
coast – one of the world's largest LNG projects. 'We're here to talk about
another way of tackling climate change, and that is capturing carbon and
storing it underground', the Prime Minister elucidated.[28] Speaking from
the facility, the Prime Minister deployed the WW storyline to help justify
a $500,000 grant from the US State Department to the Australian-led
Global Carbon Capture and Storage Institute (i.e. CCS can help enhance
economic wellbeing in developing countries that will continue to burn
fossil fuels, while ensuring environmental sustainability).[29] Soon after,
Gillard met with the US Secretary of State, Hillary Clinton, to announce
that Australia would commit up to $50 million towards the US–Australia
Solar Research Collaboration initiative, specifically designed to reduce the
cost of solar technology.[30]

   On 2 November, the Prime Minister visited Jakarta for her first bilateral
meeting with the President of Indonesia, Susilo Bambang Yudhoyono.
After the talks, both leaders agreed to work together to establish a 'global
comprehensive climate change agreement under the United Nations
Framework Convention on Climate Change' and to continue to take 'practical steps' through the Indonesia-Australia Forest Carbon Partnership to
support the Reduced Emissions from Deforestation and Degradation
(REDD) initiative.[31] The Partnership, now involving two carbon offsetting
schemes – on Sumatra and Kalimantan – totalling $70 million, 'will
further support developing the necessary policy, technical and financial
capabilities for participation in future international carbon markets for
REDD', the leaders joint statement explained.

   Australia's ultimate objective on this issue was to ensure that actions to
reduce deforestation qualified for emissions crediting under the Kyoto Protocol's (KP) Clean Development Mechanism (CDM) in a post-2012 global
deal. If Australia could convince the KP Parties to adopt REDD under the
CDM, and satisfy the relevant UNFCCC Subsidiary Body for Scientific
and Technological Advice (SBSTA) requirements, it could then use the
generated Certified Emission Reduction (CERs), or 'official' Kyoto units,
to meet part of its emissions reduction targets under the KP and offset any
competitive disadvantages industry may encounter from a national price
on carbon.

   From 11–12 November 2010, the Prime Minister attended the G20
Leaders' Meeting in Seoul, South Korea. Gillard was a keen supporter of

Australia developing a uranium export industry. At the meeting, she and President of Russia, Dmitry Medvedev, oversaw the entry into force of an agreement for Australian uranium to be exported to Russia for energy purposes. Gillard deployed the WW storyline to help legitimise the Agreement: 'The Agreement will help Russia to meet its expanding energy needs as it seeks to reduce its greenhouse emissions (as well as) increase export opportunities and create jobs for Australia's uranium suppliers', she explained.[32] Dispute this, Gillard rejected the proposition that Australia should build nuclear power stations at home: 'We don't need them. We're a country with abundant solar, wind, geothermal, tidal', she confirmed.

Next, Gillard flew to Yokohama, Japan, to attend the Asia Pacific Economic Cooperation (APEC) Leaders' Meeting held between 13–14 November. Here, Gillard met with President of Mexico, Felipe Calderon. They discussed the upcoming UNFCCC negotiations to be held in Cancun, Mexico. 'Focus will very much be on forests', explained Gillard, which suited Australia perfectly given its diplomatic endeavours on REDD.[33] At the conclusion of the talks, the APEC Leaders' Declaration stated that the leaders remain 'fully dedicated to United Nations climate change negotiations'.[34] Labor Party traditions hold that Australia's interests are best served by shaping UN processes (as Chapter 3 showed). So, centralising the UNFCCC in global climate governance, as opposed to prioritising bilateral or regional management regimes, was the critical second pillar to Australia's advocacy on REDD.

Upon her return to Australia, on 29 November, the Prime Minister delivered an important speech in which she declared that '2011 is the year Australia decides on carbon pricing'.[35] The prospective carbon pricing mechanism, Gillard explained, would need to muster 'sufficient consensus in the Parliament so that it can be legislated'. The negotiations within the MPCCC would ensure this, she suggested. It would also need to garner sufficient community support. Several upcoming business roundtables and community meetings, as well as union and environmental non-governmental organisation involvement, and the release of several high-level reports (by Ross Garnaut, the Productivity Commission and the Climate Commission) would ensure this, she added. For decision-makers, Gillard warned, 'in 2011 there will be nowhere to hide'.

But while Gillard's speech delivered clues about the process that would lead to a national price on carbon, it lacked, as was commonplace in her important speeches about climate policy, a conveyance about the high environmental costs to Australia, the region and the world of failing to reduce emissions (via a carbon pricing mechanism in this case). Therefore, this speech can be considered the third Critical Discourse Moment in the Gillard years. In its stead, Gillard increasingly deployed the localised version of economic CNTA storyline about carbon pricing halting electricity price rises.

The trouble, for Gillard, with repeatedly deploying this proximate iteration of the economic CNTA storyline was that Australia's climate debate would henceforth become fixated upon whether the Prime Minister's or the opposition leader's climate policy would increase or decrease household electricity prices. And debating cost-of-living pressures was Abbott's preferred political ground.

In response the Prime Minister's speech, the MCA's Mitch Hooke asserted that 'adequate protection for the competitiveness of coal exporters must be a central element of any new carbon pricing arrangement'. Indeed, protecting coal's competitiveness was 'in the national interest', added Hooke. For Hooke, this could be achieved were 'the Government to pursue a global agreement that includes emissions reduction commitments from all major emitting nations' as well as one that 'supports the inclusion of carbon capture and storage projects in future offset arrangements'.[36]

Ralph Hillman from the ACA took a different approach. He argued that CCS should be categorised under the carbon price similarly to other 'low emission technologies such as solar thermal and geothermal'.[37] Similarly to Hooke however, he agreed that developing CCS technology was in Australia's interests, in this instance, because once operational it could be deployed in countries that consume Australian coal which would allow Australia's coal trade to continue in relative perpetuity, he suggested.

Similarly to the MCA, for the APPEA and Belinda Robinson, a national price on carbon, she argued, must, above all else, 'maintain the competitiveness of Australian export industries, particularly cleaner global contributor exports such as LNG'. Protecting LNG exporters was in the national interest, she added. This could be achieved, the APPEA argued, by establishing a domestic carbon pricing scheme that 'recognized the widest possible range of credible offsets' and linked to a global agreement that 'allows for the unrestricted flow of credible emissions units between international jurisdictions'.[38]

In the period between 29 November 2010 and 10 December 2010, the Sixteenth Conference of the Parties (COP16) to the UNFCCC was held in Cancun, Mexico. The Prime Minister did not attend, with Australia's climate minister, Greg Combet, attending on her behalf. Here, Combet argued that the Australian government wanted progress on two fronts: the establishment of a 'comprehensive international agreement covering all emitters', particularly the US and China; and second, progress on REDD+ and the monitoring of carbon stored in forests for offsetting purposes.[39]

On 9 December, Combet announced that Australia would allocate $45 million to Indonesia to strengthen the Australia-Indonesia partnership on REDD+ activities. This new funding would help 'accelerate joint work on

Indonesia's National Carbon Accounting System (INCAS)', asserted Australia's Foreign Minister, Kevin Rudd, who also attended the COP16.[40] The INCAS system aimed to increase forest carbon monitoring and accounting capacity in Indonesia. This data could then be used to generate credits for use in Australia's domestic scheme, which went unsaid publicly.[41]

The following day, on 10 December, Combet announced that Australia would allocate $10 million to the World Bank's new Partnership for Market Readiness scheme, becoming its lead donor. Combet explained that 'The Partnership will provide a platform for policymakers and practitioners in both developed and developing countries to share knowledge of carbon markets'.[42] In other words, linking offsetting schemes across international borders. Towards the end of the COP16, speaking from Canberra, Gillard repeatedly stressed that 'As Prime Minister, I am guided each and every day about what's in our national interests ... (and) It is in the interests of Australians to get our economy ready for a low pollution future'.[43]

2011

As January commenced, the government was faced with responding to a series of enormous, and mostly unprecedented, floods across Queensland, New South Wales and Victoria. The Prime Minister downplayed their link to climate change: 'I don't think that you can look at one event and say that it equals climate change', she said.[44] By contrast, Bob Brown called for the coal industry to pay for the clean-up.[45] On 27 January 2011, Prime Minister Gillard announced that the government would be 'abolishing, differing and capping' access to a number of carbon abatement programmes on the basis that they would soon be superseded by the incoming carbon price.[46]

The following week, on 6 February 2011, Combet publicly flagged the possibility of a 'two staged scheme' – starting with a fixed price on carbon, before moving to a fully-flexible emissions trading scheme. Gillard would not confirm or deny Combet's remarks.[47] Nonetheless, the announcement spurred public debate about the level of compensation industry could expect. Greens Party Deputy Leader, Christine Milne, argued that the high level of compensation available under the CPRS – which included the allocation of billions of dollars and unlimited international offsets to the fossil fuel industry – would not cut the mustard.[48] In response, Gillard asserted: 'it's not my intention to throw all that work out the door on industry assistance'.[49]

On 24 February 2011, Gillard, Combet, Brown, Milne, Windsor, and Rob Oakeshott – another Independent member – held a press conference in the Prime Minister's courtyard, to announce that the government would introduce a carbon price effective from 1 July 2012, with a fixed price for three years, before, as Gillard described it, 'a smooth transition to a full cap and trade emissions trading scheme with a flexible price that is linked to international carbon markets' in 2015.[50] As she had done since taking office in June 2010, Gillard deployed the economic CNTA storyline, with an international orientation, to frame government climate policy: 'Australia is at risk of falling behind the rest of the world. The longer we wait, the greater cost to the economy and to Australian jobs'. She also deployed the WW storyline to help legitimate the policy, for example: our climate plan will 'cut pollution, tackle climate change and deliver the economic reform Australia needs'. Here too the economic advantages took precedent over the environmental advantages. But while the policy and the commencement date had been announced, the MPCCC had not come to an agreement on the starting price, household compensation, support for Emissions Intensive Trade Exposed (EITE) industries or the treatment of the energy sector. This information vacuum lead to wild speculation in the media.

To make matters worse, in an interview that evening, Gillard described the mechanism as a 'tax', which was a tacit acknowledgement that she had misled voters during the election campaign. 'Host: With this carbon tax – you do concede it's a carbon tax, do you not? Gillard: Oh, look, I'm happy to use the word tax.'[51] As could be expected, this concession unleashed a week of intense criticism of the Prime Minister about whether she had lied to the Australian people on election eve about her intension to introduce a carbon tax. Interviewers would play the audio: '*there will be no carbon tax under the government I lead*'. Then follow with a barrage of questions/ accusations about 'lying', 'mistrust', 'integrity', 'credibility', 'honesty', 'broken promise', and 'fibbing'.[52] Gillard sought to justify her use of the word 'tax', by arguing that she 'didn't want to get involved in a semantic debate' about whether it was a tax or a fixed price, 'so, that's why I was upfront and said it's effectively like a tax' before its moves into a cap and trade emissions trading scheme.[53] Subsequently, questions about the 'tax's' impact on cost-of-living pressures dominated Gillard's time on the airwaves as she attempted to sell the plan. 'How much will a cup of coffee go up?' 'How much will petrol go up?' she was asked. None of which she could answer with any real precision or certainty.

In response to all this, Gillard did not seek to deploy the environmental CNTA storyline or environmentally focused WW storyline to help legitimise the carbon pricing plan. Climate impacts were largely abandoned by the Prime Minister. She would simply (re)state that she believes in the science and the best way to tackle carbon pollution is to price carbon. As always, Gillard prioritised the economic, internationally orientated, CNTA storyline.

The absence of the environmental CNTA storyline during the 24 February announcement and in its aftermath, combined with Gillard conceding the notion of a 'carbon tax', can be considered the fourth Critical Discourse Moment in the Gillard years. This missed opportunity, and political misstep, had the effect of further narrowing the debate about climate policy down to the impacts that the 'tax' might have on cost-of-living pressures, which again, was squarely in Tony Abbott's political territory – his would be a 'lower taxing government', a line that he had conveyed since ascending to opposition leader in December 2009.

The ACA's response to the government's announcement 'urged the Prime Minister to preserve industry competitiveness in her proposal for a carbon tax … International competitiveness is the central issue for the coal industry in the government's proposed carbon price', Hillman pleaded in his opening sentence. As previously stated, for Hillman and the ACA, to protect coal's competitive position, fugitive (methane) emissions from coal mining operations would need to be deemed eligible for compensation, and the government would need to continue to fund CCS development. Hillman deployed the CTA storyline to delegitimate a scheme design that failed to adopt these recommendations: 'Anything that adds to Australia's cost structure diminishes the competitiveness of Australian mines and the attraction of Australia as an investment destination, and will ultimately cost jobs'.[54] For Hillman, CCS is the only WW solution to climate change for Australia: 'The development of effective low emission technologies [CCS] will permit Australia to continue to exploit its comparative advantage as a resource rich economy while reducing our greenhouse gas emissions'.[55] The MCA's response added that coal's competitiveness could only be maintained if the climate scheme offered the industry 100 per cent free permits.[56]

The APPEA's response was slightly different. Robinson argued that 'The design of Australia's carbon price must be done in a way that encourages, rather than impedes, the development of Australia's enormous gas resources.'[57] For the APPEA, this approach would yield WW results (i.e. reduce emissions compared to coal, create jobs, and support the economy).

In early March, Gillard was under siege. Polling put her personal approval rating at 30 per cent. And rising electricity prices provided easy political fodder for Tony Abbott who argued that repealing the carbon price would reduce power prices by avoiding cost imposts on electricity generators (the localised economic CTA storyline). Gillard sought to counter by arguing, as she had many times previously, that establishing a national carbon price would create business certainty and therefore encourage investment in electricity generation and thus reduce electricity prices (the localised economic CNTA storyline).[58] In mid-March Gillard visited the US. In Washington, DC, she met with the US President Barack Obama, Republican Senator John McCain, and delivered an Address to the Congress. She repeatedly deployed the WW storyline to justify Australia establishing a carbon pricing scheme, also describing it as 'in the national interest'. She also sought to build a coalition of support for carbon pricing, repeatedly identifying a list of other countries that were pricing carbon. Gillard also repeatedly mentioned the start date of Australia's scheme: '1st of July 2012'.[59] In New York, Gillard identified a list of companies that 'believe in carbon pricing'. Earlier, Gillard had met with the Prime Minister of New Zealand, John Key. New Zealand had had a national price on carbon for some time. She used New Zealand's experience as an example of a workable WW carbon pricing scheme.[60]

But while Gillard used these international meetings to advocate for her domestic climate plan, she also used them to advocate for the UNFCCC remaining central to global climate governance. For example, after meeting with the President of Mongolia, both leaders agreed that the UNFCCC process and protocols (i.e. Cancun Agreement) require 'prompt implementation'.[61] And in New York, drawing on several Labor foreign policy ideas and traditions, Gillard declared:

> We played an active and constructive role in the formation of the Cancun Agreements, which built on the Copenhagen accord. We believe in an effective and responsive United Nations. We believe in the multilateral system and its capacity to address global problems. We believe in the ideal of good global citizenship.[62]

In late March, after returning from the US, the Prime Minister deployed the economic CNTA and WW storylines to help justify the government's carbon pricing plan. Both storylines had a distinct 'jobs' focus, much more so than prior to departing to the US. For example, 'putting a price on carbon will create the right incentive to create that clean energy future. It will be good for our environment, but it will also be good for the future of Australian jobs', she would repeatedly state – speaking mostly from renewable energy enterprises.[63]

This 'jobs' focus continued into April. For Gillard, as she repeatedly explained, 'In designing this scheme we are of course going to work with industry to protect Australian jobs'. These were fossil fuel jobs. But, 'the other jobs dynamic here is the clean energy jobs that come', she would continue.[64] In short, the design would have to offer sufficient concessions to big polluters to protect current jobs, but also be sufficiently strict (on big polluters) as to incentivise the creation of low pollution industries and thus protect future jobs.

Australia's coal and gas/LNG peak bodies continued to lobby the government for particular design concessions that protected the competitive position of their corporate members. The MCA warned that it, and its members, 'will not support a carbon pricing system that fails to maintain the international competitiveness of Australia's export industries',[65] Hooke even suggesting that 'the Government should apply a No-Disadvantage to Competitiveness Test to the proposed carbon pricing scheme'.[66] Coal exporters require unlimited free permits and concessions for fugitive emissions to remain competitive, the MCA argued. Similarly, the APPEA's Robinson warned that 'Australian gas exporters must not to be disadvantaged by a policy that is unmatched in competitor countries'.[67] Dissimilarly however, the APPEA wanted gas/LNG excluded from the scheme because 'selling our gas to the world is the most meaningful thing Australia can do to reduce global emissions'.

Towards the end of April, Gillard visited Japan, Republic of Korea (ROK) and China – Australia's top destinations for Australian LNG. In the aftermath of bilateral meetings held in each capital with Prime Minister Kan of Japan, President Lee of ROK, and Premier Jiabao of China, Gillard confirmed that Australia would continue to work closely with each country to address climate change, and that Australia was committed to continuing LNG exports to these destinations.[68] Upon returning, Gillard flew to Western Australia to officially launched work on the $16 billion Santos Liquefied Natural Gas Project near Gladstone: 'This is also part of Australia and the world moving to cleaner energy sources ... when I was recently overseas in Japan, in South Korea and in China all of the talk was of Australia's ability to supply the energy sources of the future', she explained.[69]

In May, two major reports were released that deployed the environmental CNTA storyline to frame the importance of reducing emissions (via a policy mechanism). On 23 May, the Climate Council released a report titled, The Critical Decade.[70] On 31 May, Professor Ross Garnaut – a Rudd climate adviser, and adviser to the MPCCC – delivered an updated version of his ground-breaking 2008 report. Gillard did deploy the environmental CNTA storyline in this time. For example, 'our planet is warming and that has huge effects for the Australian economy in the future and for our environment in the future. I am determined that we will price carbon'.[71] Also in May, the Productivity Commission released a report titled, Carbon Emission Policies in Key Economies.[72] This report, Gillard explained:

'showed that our top trading partners are undertaking a substantial amount of action on climate change'.[73] Australia's industrial heavyweights didn't agree.

Later in May, the MCA, the ACA, and the APPEA provided submissions to the government's 'carbon price policy development process'. Protecting competitiveness was their central concern. The APPEA's front page declared, in bold – the only point that was: 'The overall package of carbon price design and associated assistance measures should take appropriate account of impacts on the competitiveness of all Australian industries'.[74] Inside, the APPEA's asserted: 'Australia's LNG projects face fierce global competition. Australia's major LNG competitors include Qatar, Indonesia, Malaysia, Trinidad & Tobago, Oman, the United Arab Emirates, Egypt, Equatorial Guinea, Nigeria, Algeria and Brunei'; but in the future could also include 'PNG, Russia and the US'.[75] Similarly the MCA's front page professed: 'An Australian carbon pricing scheme will be effective only as part of an integrated policy approach which includes a measured transition to carbon pricing, with cost burdens comparable with those facing our competitors'.[76] Inside, the MCA (and the ACA elsewhere[77]) identified Australia's major coal export competitors as, particularly Indonesia, South Africa, and Colombia; but also, the Russian Federation, Canada, the USA, and Mozambique.[78]

While each lobby group prescribed a range of design features and priorities that, if adopted by government, would help protect their competitive position, consistent across all three was the importance of the government allocating a large number of free permits. As the MCA affirmed: 'there should be a full allocation of permits to trade exposed firms', in their absence, 'the carbon tax will simply serve to undermine the economy sacrificing jobs, our international competitiveness and standard of living'.[79] Similarly for the ACA: 'to get the design of its carbon tax right and protect Australia's trade exposed jobs and industries' it should include the allocation of free permits.[80] The APPEA likewise wrote: 'a package of measures to maintain the international competitiveness of the Australian LNG industry is required, including (free) permit allocations set at and remaining at 100 per cent'.[81]

The following month, on 15 June, Gillard hit back releasing a 'Myth Busting' Fact Sheet explaining that 'Australia's top five trading partners – China, Japan, the United States, the Republic of Korea and India – and another six of our top twenty trading partners, have implemented or are piloting carbon trading or taxation schemes'.[82] She would also release a report, alongside former Australian Prime Minister, Bob Hawke, that 'warned that Kakadu – one of Australia's World Heritage Listed sites – is vulnerable to the impacts of climate change', and therefore, 'it is critically important that we take action now'.[83] Gillard also announced that 'three million lower income households will get a safety net buffer of 20 per cent more than the expected impact on them of the flow through of the carbon price'.[84] And she took aim at Australia's big polluters: 'When we price carbon, we'll know where the money's coming from, it's coming from the 1000 biggest polluters in this country'.[85]

In response, the ACA launched a series of reports that it had previously commissioned. On 8 June, the Centre for International Economics, a coal-friendly think tank, found that 'no country that competes with Australia's exporting coal mines faces a tax on fugitive emissions emitted during the process of mining coal'.[86] On 14 June, the ACIL–Tasman – another coal ally – produced economic modelling that found 'the carbon tax will put thousands of jobs at risk (3000 in Queensland and 1000 in NSW) and push billions of investment dollars in new mining developments offshore to our competitors'.[87] Based on the findings of both reports, Ralph Hillman repeatedly deployed the LL storyline to delegitimise a carbon pricing design that failed to allocate unlimited free permits and compensate for fugitive emissions.[88] For example:

> The proposed carbon tax will impose $18 billion in new costs on Australian coal mines, costs that this research confirms none of our competitors face. These increased costs will tilt the playing field in favour of our competitors resulting in job losses in Australian coal mining for no reduction in the amount of greenhouse gases emitted.[89]

Towards the end of June, Gillard started talking about the importance of coal. For example: 'I believe coal's got a future in this country and we will be delivering measures to work with the coal industry as we transition into carbon pricing'.[90]

On 4 July 2011, Gillard forecast that 'this weekend, we will announce a price on pollution as the central element of a comprehensive policy to tackle climate change'. She deployed the WW storyline to both legitimise the MPCCC negotiations and the perspective carbon pricing plan. In terms of the former, Gillard maintained that 'the MPCCC talks in recent weeks have reflected a genuine commitment to tackle climate change to protect Australia's environment and support the economy'.[91]

The following week, on 10 July 2011, the Prime Minister announced Australia's carbon pricing mechanism titled, Securing A Clean Energy Future: The Australian Government's Climate Change Plan (CEF).[92] From 1 July 2012, about 500 big polluters (down from the previously stated 1000) would be required to pay AU$23 a tonne for the carbon pollution that they emit into the atmosphere, which, Gillard elucidated 'at the movement, they do for free'.[93] The government would set the price for three consecutive years – 'this works effectively like a tax', Gillard said repeatedly.[94] It will rise 2.5 per cent each year over those years, to $24.15 per tonne in 2013, and $25.40 in 2014. On 1 July 2015, Australia will transition to a fully-flexible ETS, after which time the market will set the price, Gillard concluded.

To frame the policy, the Prime Minister deployed a perfunctory version of the CNTA storyline: 'Most Australians now agree our climate is changing, this is caused by carbon pollution, this has harmful effects on our environment and on the economy – and the Government should act'.

This statement dramatically undersold the extent to which Australia's environmental interests were under threat as a result of delayed emission reductions. Therefore, this event – the most important event on climate to date in the Gillard years – can be considered the fifth and final Critical Discourse Moment in the Gillard years. It was the final Critical Discourse Moment because from this point forward, as we shall see, the CNTA storyline to frame and justify the introduction of climate policies was subordinated to the WW storyline deployed to legitimise and 'sell' the policy itself.

At the announcement itself, the Prime Minister deploy the WW storyline to help legitimise the CEF. The environmental 'win'/advantages were operationalised in their most basic form, for example, 'By 2020, the CEF would have cut carbon pollution by 160 million tonnes a year. That's the equivalent of taking 45 million cars off the road'.[95] By contrast, the economic 'win'/advantages comprised two dimensions. The first advantage of the CEF was that it protected households,[96] pensioners[97] and low-income families[98] from potential cost increases as a result of the carbon price. The second advantage was that it protected the competitiveness of Australian industries, which took the guise of 'protecting jobs', as Gillard herself explained:

> I understand that there is nothing more important to families than having a job. So I have decided we will take special measures to support (fossil fuel) jobs and keep Australia competitive internationally. And some of the money paid by polluters will also fund billions of dollars of investments in clean technologies like solar, wind and geothermal.[99]

As this implies, under Gillard's carbon price, industry/job assistance was two-fold. The first aspect was about protecting the competitiveness of Australia's current high-polluting industries and thus protecting current jobs. The second aspect was about protecting the competitiveness of Australia's future low-polluting industries, which was important as the world decarbonises, and thus protecting future jobs.

To protect the competitiveness of Australia's fossil fuel industry, and the current jobs therein, Gillard announced a range of compensatory measures, including:

- The Jobs and Competitiveness Program, which would provide $9.2 billion over the first three years (in free permits) to 'support businesses within emissions-intensive trade-exposed industries that face international competition from companies in countries yet to introduce comparable costs on carbon'.[100]
- A Steel Transformation Plan, which would provide $300 million in addition to the 95 per cent free permits available to the steel industry 'to support jobs in Australian steel manufacturing'.[101]
- A Coal Sector Jobs Package, which would provide $1.3 billion 'to support jobs in the Australian coal industry'.[102]
- A Coal Mining Abatement Technology Support Package, which would provide $70 million 'to assist coal mines develop and deploy new technologies to reduce their carbon pollution' and jobs into the future.
- An Energy Security Fund, which would include two key initiatives to shield Australia's big polluters in the electricity sector from the carbon price. First, transitional assistance in the form of a mixture of cash payments and free carbon permits would be provided to the most emissions-intensive coal fired power stations in Australia. Second, short-term loans to generators to help finance their purchase of carbon permits and support the re-financing of existing debt if commercial loans are unavailable.[103]
- The government also linked 'gas' to the list of cleaner fuels, alongside renewables: 'The carbon price will change Australia's electricity generation by encouraging investment in renewable energy like wind and solar power, and the use of cleaner fuels like natural gas.'[104]

In terms of protecting the low pollution jobs of the future, Gillard announced a suite of new initiatives to support innovation in clean and renewable energy, including:

- A Clean Energy Finance Corporation, which would invest '$10 billion in businesses seeking funds to get innovative clean energy proposals and technologies off the ground'.[105]

In response to the announcement, the ACA's media release opened with: 'The Gillard Government's carbon tax package released today will reduce the growth of coal mining in Australia and give a free kick to Australia's coal trade competitors.' Hillman himself deployed the CTA storyline and LL storyline to delegitimise the CEF, which like the government, focused on jobs. In the first instance, for example, Hillman explained: 'the carbon tax will cost thousands of jobs in regional communities as its impact is felt on ordinary Australians'. In the second instance, for example: 'we do not support the package that was announced today which will put 4700 miners out of work and do nothing to reduce global emissions'.[106]

The MCA's Mitch Hooke also deployed the LL storyline: 'The Government-Greens carbon tax package announced today is a very poor investment in our environmental and economic future.' Hooke's central criticism however, was that it failed to protect the competitive position of the fossil fuel industry: 'It will impose the highest carbon price in the world, compromising the competitiveness of Australia's export competing sectors without environmental benefit.'[107]

The APPEA also deployed the LL storyline in an attempt to delegitimise the CEF on the basis that LNG exports were not exempt compared to domestic gas: 'the carbon policy announced today recognises the role of gas within Australia but does little to protect the competitiveness of Australia's gas export industry', and on this basis, 'today's announcement hurts the industry's competitiveness, without decreasing net global emissions'.[108]

But while the CEF had been announced, it would need to pass through the Parliament before it would become law. This meant that the coal and gas lobbies still had time to shape the outcome to serve the interests of their members – as Hillman put it: 'The carbon tax is just a proposal at this stage and before it becomes law we believe there is still a chance to get the government to reconsider some of the more detrimental elements of the tax'.[109] The government knew this, and set about selling the CEF to the Australian people.

For the remainder of July, and also in August – covering the period of time from the above announcement to when the legislation was introduced into the House of Representatives – Gillard toured the country selling the CEF. She stressed that the carbon price was a balanced scheme insofar that it protected Australia's economic and environmental interests – it was a WW Plan, she repeatedly argued. The notion of balancing economic and environmental imperatives, in practice, translated into on one day Gillard visiting a coal mining community and repeatedly stating that coal has a 'big', 'good', or 'great' future in Australia, and to rest assured that Australia will continue to burn coal domestically as well as export coal, which will protect Australian jobs. While on the following day, she would visit a wind or solar facility and repeatedly state that these enterprises will generate the clean energy jobs of the future.[110]

The government's WW storyline was supported by the release of Treasury modelling on the carbon price, which, similarly to the Prime Minister, focused on the economic advantages, and particularly 'jobs'. Titled, Strong Growth, Low Pollution (the WW storyline), the report showed that 'incomes and jobs will increase substantially while our country takes action to reduce the risks of dangerous climate change'. The modelling also deployed the economic CNTA storyline: 'delaying action on climate change will only lead to dramatically higher costs, will undermine our competitiveness and will ultimately hit jobs and living standards'.[111]

The environmental win/advantages however would soon come under fire. To sell the environmental integrity of the CEF, Gillard repeatedly claimed that the carbon price on roughly 500 big polluters 'will cut carbon pollution by 160 million tonnes in 2020, the equivalent of 45 million vehicles'. But, the trouble was, 100 million tonnes of the 160 million would come by buying permits from offshore. Unrepentant, Gillard repeatedly responded in the following way (or similarly):

> Yes, this is going to be an internationally linked scheme and so it should be. I want our economy to transform to a clean energy economy and I want us to cut carbon pollution at the lowest possible cost and international linking is part of having the lowest possible cost. It's the way you protect Australian businesses, the way you protect international competitiveness and therefore protect Australian jobs. Anyone who is telling you that they don't want an internationally linked scheme is saying to Australians, 'Do this for a higher cost than you need to pay'. Why should we pay more to get the job done of cutting carbon pollution than we need to? Why on earth would you do that?

Gillard believed that permits would avoid firms moving offshore.

> So from 1 July 2015, there'll be a 'cap and trade' market creating the incentive to cut pollution at the lowest cost. I knew there was no environmental benefit in emissions intensive, trade exposed production simply moving offshore. So, we will allocate some permits to some businesses without charge, supporting jobs and competitiveness, and helping strongly affected industries make the transition to a clean energy future. I also wanted to link our carbon price to the emerging international market, keeping Australian industry competitive. So Australian business will be to be able to buy permits which represent credible, additional, offshore pollution reductions.[112]

For the remainder of July and August, the coal lobby too toured the country, but in contrast to the government, they deployed the CTA and LL storylines to delegitimise the CEF. On 18 July 2011, the ACA launched a television advertising campaign to 'highlight the regional impact of the carbon tax'.[113] The coal industry had not gotten what it wanted on fugitive emissions, which meant the scheme was a LL one, they argued: 'Australian government is the only government in the world to tax fugitive emissions from coal mining, threatening our international competitiveness and costing Australian jobs – but with no impact on global greenhouse emissions'.[114] To pressure the government into altering the CEF design before it became law Hillman repetitively deployed the CTA storyline, operationalised at a local level, to delegitimise the CEF, for example, 'The Hunter Valley, like many of Australia's coal mining communities, will feel the hit the economy is expected to take with the introduction of the carbon tax' – Hillman gave accompanying examples and figures of expected mines closures, local job losses in the thousands, small business closures, and cited the ACIL report as evidence of these 'costs'. The ACA also targeted regional Queensland, deploying the same storylines but with substituted examples and figures relating to Queensland's coal mining regions.[115]

On 21 July 2011, the MCA announced that it had joined with the ACA, and five other industry groups, to conduct a nation-wide advertising campaign to 'provide fact-based information on the impact of the carbon tax on trade-exposed business competitiveness, economic and employment growth and prices'.[116] The campaign slogan, 'Carbon Tax Pain. No Climate Change Gain', deployed the LL storyline too, as the media release stated, 'highlight the futility of the Government's proposed scheme. It will impose massive costs for no material environmental dividend'.[117] Before the CEF becomes law, the industry coalition urged, the government must alter its design to ensure 'the scheme does not compromise the competitiveness of Australia's export and import competing industries'. The MCA also released commissioned modelling by Deloitte Access Economics (DAE) that found that 'the minerals industry is expected to pay a record $23.4 billion in taxes and royalties to Federal and State Governments in 2010–2011', which was under threat by the proposed carbon tax design.[118]

Yet despite this strong showing from the fossil fuel lobby, resignations precipitated the CEF announcement. On 28 July 2011, the APPEA announced that Belinda Robinson, who had been APPEA Chief since 2005, would be replaced by former ExxonMobile executive, David Byers. On 22 August 2011, the ACA announced that Ralph Hillman, who had been ACA Chief since 2007 (and Australia's Ambassador for the Environment and chief negotiator for Australia on the Kyoto Protocol from 1998 to 2002), would be replaced by the Chief of the Minerals Council of New

South Wales, Nikki Williams (but as we shall see ACA Chairman, John Pegler, would do most of the public advocacy). Mitch Hooke would continue in his role as CEO of the Minerals Council of Australia.

In the final week before the CEF bills were scheduled to be introduced into the House of Representatives, Gillard shared the stage with several international political heavy hitters, all of whom deployed the, rarely seen, environmental CNTA storyline to justify the passage of the CEF legislation. On 3 September, Gillard hosted UN Secretary General, Ban ki-Moon. Moon, a long-term advocate for emissions reductions globally, explained in a joint press conference with the Prime Minister that Australia and the region were highly vulnerable to the physical impacts of climate change.[119] On 5 September, Gillard and the EU President, José Manuel Barroso, agreed that urgent action was required to limit warming to 2 degrees Celsius.[120] The following day, 6 September, Gillard arrived in Auckland for the Pacific Island Forum. On this occasion, Gillard herself deployed a strong version of the environmental CNTA storyline:

> Anybody who's in any doubt about the devastating effects of climate change should have a conversation with President of Kiribati. They are living with it every day in a nation that is so at risk from rising sea levels. We need to act to cut carbon pollution. We need to do that because it's the right thing to do by the environment, but also to secure clean energy jobs. That's what putting a price on carbon is all about. The legislation will go through and carbon will be priced from the 1st of July next year.[121]

In the following week, on 13 September, the *Clean Energy Bill 2011*, was introduced into the House of Representatives. In her speech in the House to accompany the bill, the Prime Minister deployed a much lighter version of the CNTA storyline than the week prior, simply conveying the basic climate science (about warming, causes, and impacts) to justify the passage of the bill through the Parliament. Gillard also deployed the WW storyline to serve the same end: on the one hand, the implementation of the bill would allow for compensation to be delivered to households and businesses, and on the other hand, result in the removal of '160 million tonnes' of carbon pollution from the atmosphere by 2020.[122]

The coal lobby continued to deploy the CTA storyline to push for amendments to the proposed legislation so that it would better protect the competitive position of their corporate members. To that effect, as the bill was debated in the House, both the MCA and the ACA released commissioned reports on expected job losses. The MCA's report found that 'less than 9 per cent of Australia's 1.05 million manufacturing employees are employed by firms likely to receive assistance under the Jobs and Competitiveness Program'.[123] The result was expressed in the title of the media release that accompanied the report: '950,000 Manufacturing Workers Fully Exposed to World's Biggest Carbon Tax'.[124] The ACA's 'definitive' report found that 'The carbon tax will put at risk over 21,000 jobs, cause over 20 mine closures in NSW and Queensland, and threaten new mining enterprises'.[125]

This was shortly followed, on 26 September, by submissions by the ACA and the APPEA to the Joint Select Committee on Australia's Clean Energy Future Legislation.[126] The central message expressed in the submissions from both the coal and gas/LNG industry was that the legislation must, above all else, protect the competitive position of Australia mining vis-à-vis foreign countries. Both submissions were replete with expressions of urgent concern about the current bill undermining Australia's industrial competitiveness.

Also in September (and throughout 2011) the Gillard Government lodged a series of submissions to the UNFCCC on behalf of Australia. In the submissions, the government argued that CCS and REDD should be included under the CDM for offsetting purposes. For example, 'Australia welcomes the inclusion of CCS as an eligible project activity under the CDM' read one submission.[127] While on REDD, Australia lodged a joint submission with Indonesia[128] as well as an individual submission,[129] and two separate submissions about the importance of measuring, reporting, and verifying forest offsets.[130]

On 12 October, the *Clean Energy Bill 2011* passed the House of Representatives 74 votes to 72. The MCA immediately deployed the LL storyline: 'The Parliament has voted to reduce Australia's standard of living, undermine the competitiveness of export and import competing businesses and cut domestic jobs growth for no climate change gain.'[131] As did the ACA: 'Our view has not changed. The carbon tax will undermine the competitiveness of Australian coal mines with no reduction in the amount of global greenhouse gas emissions from coal mining'.[132] Later in day, on 12 October, the *Clean Energy Bill* was introduced into the Australian Senate.

As the bills were debated in the Senate, the Prime Minister was out and about deploying the WW storyline, as always, the economic advantages took precedent (i.e. households and industry will not be out of pocket as a result of pricing carbon, there will be tax cuts and more money for low-income families, industry compensation, and clean energy jobs).

On 8 November 2011, the Australian Senate passed the Clean Energy Future package of 18 bills without amendment, and it would become the *Clean Energy Act 2011*. Triumphant, the Prime Minister declared:

Today's vote is a win for Australia's children, it's a win for those who will seek their fortune and make their way by having jobs in our clean energy sector. It's a win for those who want our environment to be a cleaner environment and to see less carbon pollution. Today we have made history. After all of these years of debate and division our nation has got the job done and from the 1st of July we will see a price on carbon pollution. I've made the decisions in the nation's interests.[133]

The coal lobby conveyed its disappointment by deploying the CTA and LL storyline. For the ACA, 'the legislation passed today means a package of measures with fatal flaws becomes law'. The first was the exclusion of fugitive emissions from coal mining from compensation (and enshrining coal's exclusion in legislation). 'No other coal exporting country imposes a tax on fugitive emissions from coal mining', the ACA wrote, and 'In doing so, the carbon tax will make Australia's coal industry less competitive internationally, without delivering any environmental benefit by way of global emissions reduction'. The second 'fatal flaw' was that the legislation excluded CCS from funding streams available to wind and solar. The exclusion of CCS undermines 'national energy security and national competitiveness' and is 'completely inconsistent with the national interest', the ACA remonstrated.[134]

The MCA's response warned that 'The passage of the world's biggest carbon tax legislation through the Senate today and the modelling on which it is based is deeply flawed'. Again, the LL storyline was central to delegitimising the now law: 'The failure to align the carbon tax with international efforts to reduce emissions means that the environmental benefits of the scheme will be illusory, while the costs on all Australians will be very real'.[135]

Now that Australia's domestic climate scheme was in place, Australia's climate diplomacy could take on a sharper focus. And that focus was, as Labor traditions insist, to shape UN processes to serve Australia's interests. The UNFCCC negotiations in Durban were on the horizon, set for December.

In the interim, several major international events occurred without much fanfare from the Prime Minister on climate change apart from promoting Australia's domestic scheme and the UNFCCC process: for example, she did so at the Commonwealth Heads of Government Meeting held in Perth on 24 October 2011;[136] at the G20 held in Cannes on 4 November;[137] as well as at the APEC Leaders' Summit held in Honolulu on 11 November.[138] At the East Asia Summit held in Bali on 20 November, Prime Minister Gillard met with President Yudhoyono of Indonesia. Unlike at the previous events, building momentum for forest offsetting activities to be included under the UNFCCC mechanisms was a key focus, as the Joint Communique explains: Australia and Indonesia 'reaffirmed our cooperation through the International Forest Carbon Initiative to help reduce emissions from deforestation and forest degradation in developing countries ... and collaborate closely in the lead up to COP17 in Durban'.[139] A few days later, on 25 November, Australia's climate minister, Greg Combet, outlined what Australia's priorities would be at the UNFCCC negotiations in Durban.

From 1 July 2015, Australia will link its emissions trading scheme to international carbon markets. Australian companies will be allowed to use recognised international carbon units to meet their obligations. Using international permits will nearly halve the cost of meeting Australia's emissions reduction commitments in 2020.

A key national interest is the continued development of the international carbon market. One source of credits that companies in Australia will access is the United Nations Clean Development Mechanism, or CDM. Building on the CDM, Australia is also helping develop new market mechanisms. One of these – known as a REDD+ mechanism – would generate carbon credits by reducing the deforestation and forest degradation in developing countries.

From Australia's point of view, now that we have legislated for a carbon price, one of our most important goals on the international climate change stage is to ensure our businesses have access to carbon markets.

In conclusion, The Government's Clean Energy Future plan enables Australia to do its fair share. And it does so with a clear-eyed view of Australia's national interests, including a strong economy that continues to enhance our prosperity.

As Australia engages internationally at Durban and beyond, a key priority is to continue to develop the carbon markets that will enable countries everywhere to meet their pollution reduction targets at least cost.[140]

On 28 November, the Seventeen Conference of the Parties (COP17) to the UNFCCC commenced in Durban, South Africa. Gillard did not attend. Combet, who arrived in Durban on 6 December 2011, represented Australia at the talks. The following day, Combet delivered Australia's national statement, in which he declared that 'Australia will be part of a second commitment period only if it is a part of a wider agreement covering all major emitters. We have this approach because we are committed to an *environmentally effective outcome.* [emphasis added]'[141]

Combet's public presentations in Durban were saturated with the idea of Australia's ongoing participation being subject to an 'environmentally effective outcome', which simply meant a deal that included the US and China as well as Australia's trade competitors. At the COP, Combet repeatedly identified three interrelated features, which he repeatedly called 'building blocks', that would give effect to an 'environmentally friendly outcome'. First, progress on discussions, and ultimately the inclusion, of REDD+ activities under the CDM for offsetting purposes (which was the focus of the Cancun talks the previous year). Second, progress on transparency and accounting issues for REDD+ projects. Third, progress towards establishing international and regional carbon markets. 'The most important priority for Australia is the discussion with other like-minded countries of how we further carbon markets internationally', Combet explained, 'Obviously with introducing our own emissions trading scheme, we'd be looking to link that scheme to others internationally.'[142]

Gillard and Combet believed that striking an 'environmentally effective outcome' would protect Australia's national interests, which for Gillard meant protecting current jobs in the fossil fuel industry as well as those future jobs in low pollution industries. In the first instance, the only way a 'environmentally effective outcome' was attainable, as Gillard and Comet understood it, was to include REDD+ projects under the CDM (and have the projects themselves accurately measured and verified), which would permit developing countries, particularly Australia to import cheap 'official' offsets to minimise any potential economic and industrial disruption caused by a price on carbon (in short, to protect the competitive position of Australia's fossil fuel industry). In the second instance, striking an 'environmentally effective outcome' would, at least in theory, mean countries would continue to transition their economies, in a coordinated fashion, towards deploying low pollution technologies. This latter consideration would also serve Australia's environmental interests as one of the world's most vulnerable developed countries to climate impacts.

On 12 December 2011, Combet announced the outcome of the talks.[143] Australia's objectives had been satisfied. First, 'developing countries, including China, have agreed that along with developed economies, including the US, that we'll all be in the same deal and it would take effect in 2020 – the negotiations are planned to be concluded by 2015 in Paris'. Second, progress had been made on the REDD+ mechanism. Third, as Combet explained:

> The Durban decisions will encourage expansion of carbon markets which cut emissions at the lowest cost. Kyoto Protocol rules will

continue to provide for market mechanisms like the Clean Development Mechanism. The Clean Development Mechanism generates carbon credits which Australian businesses will be able to access under the Clean Energy Act's carbon price mechanism.[144]

Upon his return to Australia, Combet's portfolio responsibilities were expanded to include industry.[145]

2012

As January 2012 rolled round, Gillard was confronted with dreadful personal and party approval ratings. Abbott's relentless campaign against 'the world's biggest carbon tax' was taking its toll. ALCOA, a major aluminium smelting company, had announced it was reconsidering the viability of its ongoing operations. Some commentators were suggesting that Gillard would need to scrap the 'tax' to remain Prime Minister. 'What you're suggesting would actually risk long-term jobs and prosperity for this nation', Gillard responded.[146]

This all came to a head on 22 February 2012 with the Foreign Minister, Kevin Rudd, resigning from the Cabinet. Gillard announced that a leadership spill would take place on 27 February. In the intervening days (23–27 February), Gillard repeatedly deployed the WW storyline on carbon pricing to justify to her Party Room colleagues why she should remain Prime Minister. Rudd argued that he would move the ETS start date forward and openly accused Gillard of arguing to him that the CPRS should be shelved. Gillard responded in kind, on the first point, 'I am absolutely convinced that the legislation is right',[147] and on the second point, 'I am happy to be judged about my credibility on carbon pricing – I got it done. Didn't talk about it. Got it done. Kevin Rudd, when the going got tough he couldn't get carbon pricing done.'[148] On 27 February 2012, Rudd challenged Gillard to the leadership of the Labor Party and the Prime Ministership. Gillard won convincingly, 71 votes to 31 votes.

In the period between March and June, Gillard spent her time fending off what she described as Abbott's 'horror stories' about the impact of the carbon price. Gillard repeatedly explained that once the price was introduced and operational after 1 July 2012 all of Abbott's stories/fear campaign would be proven untrue, for example:

the public will be able to judge 'has the Sunday roast gone up by $100 as has been claimed?' The answer to that will be no. They'll be able to judge 'has my grocery shop gone up by twenty per cent?' The answer to that will be no. They'll be able to judge 'has the coal industry completely shut down around the country?', and the answer to that will certainly be no.[149]

Gillard also continued to deploy the WW storyline to justify her government's carbon pricing legislation:

> I understand that there is some anger about the decision I made to put a price on carbon. But I made the right decision in the nation's interests. It's the right decision for our economy, the right decision by our environment.[150]

She found support abroad. After bilateral talks with the Prime Minister of New Zealand, John Key, both agreed that carbon pricing was the 'most environmentally effective and economically efficient way to reduce greenhouse gas emissions'.[151] On 21 June Gillard arrived in Rio de Janeiro for the Rio+20 Conference. In a joint statement at the Conference, UNSG Ban ki-Moon said Australia was 'leading by example' on climate policy.[152] Shortly after, President of Brazil Dilma Rousseff and Gillard identified climate change as a 'priority area of cooperation'.[153] And the Conference itself produced a non-binding document titled The Future We Want, agreed to by all 192 member states (including Australia), that stressed the urgent need to tackle climate change.[154]

On 13 April, leader of the Australian Greens Party, Bob Brown, announced his retirement. His Deputy Christine Milne became leader.

Australia's price on carbon pollution commenced on 1 July 2012. On the one hand, 'The carbon price, which starts today, means that in the year 2020, Australia's carbon pollution will be at least 159 million tonnes less per annum than it would be without this policy'. On the other hand, the Prime Minister continued, families and low-income households will be compensated for price rises that business pass on to consumers, so too will heavy polluting industry – as the Prime Minister emphasised:

> The Government is also supporting jobs and competitiveness in industries with high emissions and strong international competition. The most emissions-intensive and trade-exposed industry activities are shielded from 94.5 per cent of the carbon price – meaning their effective carbon price is less than $1.30 a tonne. This will preserve international competitiveness while maintaining incentives to invest in cleaner technologies.[155]

The gas/LNG and coal lobby responded to the state date in unison, in contrast to the Prime Minister, warning that the carbon price would undermine the international competitiveness of the industrial enterprises of their respective polluting members, and therefore threaten future investment, jobs and government revenue. For example, David Byers' opening sentence of the APPEA's media release asserted: 'The commencement today of the carbon pricing mechanism represents an addition to the cost structure of Australian liquefied natural gas (LNG) exporters competing in global markets'.[156] Similarly Mitch Hooke's opening sentences of the MCA (and ACA combined) media release asserted:

> At a time of global economic uncertainty, the carbon tax erodes the minerals industry's international competitiveness. Australia should be seeking to maximise the benefits of the boom, not putting new hurdles in the way of growth in investment, exports and jobs.[157]

In early July, Gillard was scathing of the opposition leader's CTA campaign, which was designed to delegitimise the carbon price, repeatedly declaring that it had proven to be untrue, 'Australians can look around and see the sky hasn't fallen in', Gillard remarked.[158] The trouble was that for Gillard, and for Labor, nearly every price rise in the economy henceforth could be blamed on the carbon price. And electricity prices, which had been increasing for some time, were an easy target for the opposition.

In July and August, Australia's climate change debate had devolved to an argument about the impact of the carbon price on electricity prices. Gillard openly admitted that the carbon price would add 10 per cent to electricity prices, but Australians had been compensated for this.[159] She also blamed the rises on electricity transmission providers who had overinvested in polls and wires 'the so-called gold-plating of the network',[160] and the State governments who had allowed providers to do this – Abbott described this explanation as a 'fabrication'.

In subsequent months, the leaders of New South Wales, Queensland, South Australia and Western Australia raised concerns about power price rises. Gillard acknowledged that 'electricity bills have been skyrocketing. People have seen 40, 50, 60 per cent increases. But that is not about carbon pricing', rather blaming gold plating again.[161] To address these rises, Gillard worked through the Council of Australian Government (COAG) meeting.[162] But serious political damage had been done, some commentators suggesting Labor now faced 'electoral wipe-out'.

In terms of climate diplomacy in this period, on the one hand, Gillard significantly toned down her language at multilateral events about the importance of carbon pricing compared to the period of time before the price start. For example, on 31 August, Gillard attended the 2012 Pacific Island Forum on the Cook Islands, where she focused on regional adaptation.[163] On 9–10 September, she attended APEC in Vladivostok, Russia. She did not mention climate change. On 26 September, the Prime Minister delivered an Address to the UNGA in New York, which only devoted one line to climate change: 'Climate change threatens the secure food supply which guarantees development – new clean sources of energy deliver a new source of economic growth'.[164]

But on the other hand, she cultivated several bilateral relationships to advance Australia's mining resources industry. In October, the Prime Minister celebrated Australia–Japan relations by declaring that 'Australia supplies 60 per cent of Japan's iron ore and coal, and now an ever-growing proportion of its LNG'.[165] The following week, the Prime Minister visited India. On 17 October 2012, Gillard explained 'Prime Minister Dr Manmohan Singh and I have agreed that we will commence negotiations for the civil nuclear cooperation agreement, given Australia is now prepared to sell uranium to India'.[166] In India, Gillard also met with billionaire coal miner, Gautam Adani, who had proposed to build the world's largest coalmine in Queensland. 'Australia welcomed the interest of both private and public sector companies from India in the resources sector', wrote an India–Australia joint statement,[167] suggesting that Australia would give the mine consideration.

In October and November, the Gillard Government lodged two submissions to the UNFCCC. The submissions argued that Australia's involvement in a second period of the Kyoto Protocol was conditional on REDD activities being included under the CDM. The first submission addressed the issue of 'non-permanency' of forestry activities. Australia was concerned that this issue may thwart the chances of REDD activities being included under the CDM and thus generating Certified Emission Reductions (CERs) in the post-2012 period. Australia's submission stressed that 'the potential for reversal associated with the sequestration of carbon can be adequately managed through CDM', and identified a number of options including the host Party (usually a developing country) being made 'responsible for restoring carbon or handing-back CERs equivalent to the same value as the net carbon which has been credited under the project'. Ultimately, Australia's first submission concluded, options need to be canvassed as to 'provide an adequate approach to non-permanence that facilitates the issuance of fully-fungible and permanent CERs'.[168] The other submission confirmed that Australia would join a second commitment period of the Kyoto Protocol conditional on, among other things, 'access to the Kyoto market mechanisms, including the Clean Development Mechanism from 1 January 2013'.[169]

From 26 November to 8 December 2012, the Eighteenth Conference of the Parties (COP18) to the UNFCCC was held in Doha, Qatar. Here, the

Gillard Government signed up Australia to a second commitment period of the Kyoto Protocol, which would commence in 2013 and conclude in 2020. In doing so, Australia had committed to reduce its emissions by 5 per cent below 2000 levels by the year 2020. Combet's media release on this topic explained the advantage of signing up in the following way:

> Being part of Kyoto will ensure Australian businesses have guaranteed access to international credits under the Clean Development Mechanism, helping Australia to reduce carbon pollution at the lowest cost to the economy.[170]

In the latter months of 2012, the gas/LNG and coal lobbies released a series of reports that highlighted their concern about the sliding international competitiveness of their respective industries as a result of the carbon price commencing. The APPEA's 'State of the Industry 2012' Report of November 2012 wrote: 'The introduction of carbon pricing in Australia from 1 July 2012 *has* reduced the competitiveness of Australia's LNG industry by imposing a large new cost not borne by overseas competitors.'[171] Preceding this report, the APPEA released a series of reports by Deloitte titled 'Advancing Australia: Harnessing our Comparative Energy Advantage' that 'outlined the scale and significance of the Australian oil and gas industry's economic contribution' and 'flags a raft of policy areas that threaten both Australia's attractiveness as a place to do business'.[172] Similarly, in September 2012 the MCA released a report titled 'Opportunity at Risk: Regaining our Competitive Edge in Minerals Resources'.

To accompany these reports of November and September 2012, David Byers and Mitch Hooke issued media releases, which delivered remarkably similar messages. For David Byers, 'the report shows that future projects could generate large economic and tax revenue benefits for the nation for decades to come'. For Hooke: 'The prize for getting the framework for minerals resource development right is immense'. But, Byers continued, 'Australia's high-cost environment and the emergence of new LNG competitors in North America, East Africa and elsewhere will make it much harder to win market share and attract investment than has been the case over recent years'. Similarly, Hooke explained: 'Australia's costs crisis … and Australia increasing vulnerability to competition from resource-rich emerging economies means our country's attractiveness as a place to do business in a highly globalised industry is slipping.' Both Byers and Hooke agreed on the antidote – government and industry working together to protect industrial competitiveness: As Byers explained: 'To attract further investment Australia must maintain its international competitiveness.… To maintain competitiveness and secure future investment, it is critical that the industry and government work together.' Similarly, for Hooke, 'it will take hard work from both industry and government to secure the economic opportunity that is currently at risk'.[173]

2013

In January 2013, Gillard pointed to a series of events that seemed to justify her Clean Energy Act. Wildfires raged across Tasmania, New South Wales and Victoria, 'and that's why we're reducing the amount of carbon pollution we're putting up there', Gillard remarked.[174] A range of businesses were beginning to reduce emissions. Abbott's 'scare campaign' had proven manifestly false. And to usher in his second term as US President, Barack Obama delivered an inaugural Address which emphasised the urgent need to tackle climate change. Gillard was brimming with confidence. On 30 January, she announced that a Federal Election would take place on 14 September 2013.[175]

Abbott responded immediately: 'this election will be about trust'.[176] Gillard's interviews were subsequently awash with the 'there will be no carbon tax' grab. Abbott himself set this ball in motion: 'Australians will never forget that phrase that will haunt this government and this Prime Minister to its political grave: "There will be no carbon tax under the government I lead"'. Gillard was immediately on the back foot.

In addition, Abbott mercilessly deployed the CTA storyline to delegitimise the carbon price. For Abbott, the 'hated carbon tax' had cost jobs, hurt families and damaged communities, increased the cost of living, stalled investment, and was responsible, almost solely, for electricity price rises. The opposition leader believed that all this could be reserved if he was elected Prime Minister and therefore given a mandate to fulfil his 'solemn promise to the Australian people' to repeal the carbon pricing legislation as his first act in government. Indeed, 'this coming election is a referendum on the carbon tax', Abbott repeatedly declared.[177]

Abbott also repeatedly deployed the LL storyline to delegitimise the carbon price (and to justify repealing it), for example, 'The problem with the carbon tax is that it's damaged our economy without helping our environment and that's why it will go as the first priority of an incoming Coalition government'. By contrast, he deployed the WW storyline to legitimise his climate policy – described as Direct Action: 'We'll reduce emissions by planting more trees, delivering better soils and using smarter technology rather than a carbon tax that just sends our jobs overseas'.

Gillard attempted to counter Abbott's CTA storyline by deploying the economic and even environmental CNTA storylines, for example, in the first instance, citing Barack Obama's State of The Union Address of 12

February, which called for market-based solutions to climate change. 'What this just goes to show is that in pricing carbon, we are moving in the direction the world is moving'.[178] And in the second instance, for example, the Prime Minister cited the many climate-related emergences occurring across Australia, declaring 'we are now living through climate change'.[179]

But tensions were high behind the scenes in the Labor Party. Gillard was polling very poorly with the electorate. Questions about broken promises and lying were omnipresent in the media. Abbott's 'Axe the Tax' mantra was cutting through. Accusations of 'captain's picks' emerged – decisions made without consulting the Cabinet. Ministers resigned. Claims that Gillard was running a dysfunction government seemed real. Alliances were shifting behind the scenes in the Party. All this came to a head on 21 March 2013 when at 1:00 pm former Labor leader Simon Crean called for a vote on all Labor leadership positions and that he would support Kevin Rudd's return to the Prime Ministership. Gillard called for a leadership ballot at 4:30 pm. She won unopposed. The following day several Ministers resigned. Rudd announced that he would never again return as Labor leader.

In April, Gillard departed for Beijing to meet with President Xi Jinping of China. While in China, she lumped praise on Australia's 'market-based mechanism' and encouraged China to scale-up their provincial schemes to a nation-wide scheme. Indeed, 'many Asian countries' are pricing carbon, she added. Later, Gillard met with former Governor of California, Arnold Schwarzenegger: 'The Governor – a Republican – led California to put in a price on carbon to reduce carbon pollution', she explained.[180] But the main game on climate policy was occurring in Europe.

In late January, the EU Emissions Trading Scheme (EUETS) saw its carbon price fall to a record low of $3 dollars a tonne (down from $30 dollars a tonne in 2011) as a consequence of a vote in Brussels opposing support measures for the troubled scheme.[181] Australia's carbon price was set to be linked to the EUETS price after July 2015 when the scheme transitioned from a fixed price to a floating price and ETS. Gillard suggested that the EU's price may rise again by 2015, but the trouble was that the Treasury had modelled the EU price at $29 a tonne in 2015, which meant that budget forecasts could be claimed to be significantly inaccurate. In May, Gillard conceded that Australia's carbon price would probably be $12 dollars a tonne, not $29, in 2015.[182] Abbott urged the repeal of this 'toxic tax'. Speculation mounted that Rudd would again challenge for the leadership.

In the morning of 26 June 2013 it was reported that Rudd supporters were circulating a petition among Labor parliamentarians calling for a leadership ballot. Gillard had not been shown the petition. She called a snap leadership ballot for 7:00 pm that evening. Wanting to end the leadership speculation once and for all, Gillard forewarned: 'I believe anybody who enters the ballot tonight should do it on the following conditions: if you win, you're Labor leader; if you lose, you retire from politics.'[183] Kevin Rudd won the leadership spill 57 votes to 45 votes, and was thus returned as Labor leader and as Prime Minister. On 26 June 2013 at 9:30 pm, Gillard delivered her final speech as Prime Minister, climate change topped the list of achievements:

> I am proud of what this government has achieved ... I am very pleased that we pushed through and put a price on carbon – an historic reform that will serve this nation well and which required us to have the guts and tenacity to stare down one of the most reckless fear campaigns in this nation's history.[184]

Kevin Rudd's return

On 27 June 2013, Kevin Rudd was sworn-in as Prime Minister of Australia, again. In his first press conference, he confirmed that he wanted to bring forward the start date of Australia's ETS (from 1 July 2015 to 1 July 2014), having suggested it earlier in the year, but would need to consult with Cabinet colleagues first.[185] On 1 July 2013, Rudd's Cabinet was announced with Mark Butler becoming Minister responsible for climate change.[186] Also on this day Australia's fixed price on carbon entered its second year, increasing from $23 per tonne to $24.15 per tonne. Rudd's response was to argue that the government's fixed price on carbon, with its 'transparent' compensation measures, places less of a cost impost on businesses and consumers compared to Abbott's 'mysterious' Direct Action Plan.[187]

Two weeks later, on 14 July, the Prime Minister confirmed that the Cabinet was indeed working on a plan for an early transition to a floating price/ETS. Rudd repeatedly deployed the WW storyline to justify an early transition, for example: 'The Government is moving in this direction because a floating price takes cost-of-living pressures off Australian families, and still protects the environment and acts on climate change'.[188] By contrast, the Prime Minister repeatedly deployed the LL storyline to delegitimise the opposition leader's Direct Action scheme, for example: 'As for his so-called direct action model, it won't work (reduce emissions) and it will cause a huge, huge financial impost on Australian business'.[189]

Two days later, on 16 July 2013, speaking from the Great Barrier Reef, Prime Minister Rudd – accompanied by Treasurer Wayne Swan and climate minister, Mark Butler – announced that 'The Government has decided to terminate the carbon tax.'[190] If re-elected, 'from 1 July next year Australia will move to an emissions trading scheme', asserted the Prime Minister. The central justification for this transition was that it would 'help ease cost-of-living pressures for families and reduce costs for small business' as well as ensure Australia is 'playing its part to protect the environment from the effects of climate change'. In contrast to earlier deployments of the WW storyline, Rudd now had figures, generated by the Treasury, that showed that his ETS plan would cost families less compared to his opponent's plan, for example: 'The Government's new ETS will leave average families $380 per year better off, while Mr Abbott's scheme, once fully implemented will leave average families at least $1200 a year worse off'. Rudd also spoke to the environmental advantages in the following way: 'It's also good for the environment. We don't want our kids and grandkids to be able to just read about the Great Barrier Reef in some history book.'[191] At the press conference, Mark Butler also repeatedly deployed the WW storyline to legitimise the early transition.

In addition to families and the environment, Rudd, Swan, and Butler all argued that the early transition to an ETS would better protect the competitive position of Australia's fossil fuel. How would it do this?

- First, the actual carbon price would fall significantly, Rudd repeatedly declared – including in an interview on 17 July 2013 from Queensland's massive coal port in Gladstone: 'moving towards a floating carbon price is expected to reduce the carbon price from $25.40 a tonne by next July down to around $6 a tonne', which is good for families 'but it's also about providing more competitiveness for our businesses'.[192] Regarding the price fall, Mark Butler added: 'In terms of the 370 emissions intensive trade-exposed liable businesses under the ETS, they'll see a 75 per cent reduction in their carbon price liability based on where we think the price will be.'[193]
- Second, there would be 'no reduction in funding to the Jobs and Competitiveness Program which supports trade-exposed emissions intensive industries', as the Treasurer asserted.[194] Butler elaborated on this point (and the last):

> As the Treasurer said, we've also decided to keep in place entirely the assistance to those industries which are emissions intensive – so produce a lot of carbon pollution – but are also trade exposed, for the reason we don't want to see them simply close down and move to some other countries. So those free permits, up to 92 per cent of free permits, will also remain untouched. Plus, a carbon

price that is reduced by 75 per cent. So if anything, those industries are significantly better off as a result of our decision to terminate the carbon tax.[195]

For the coal and gas/LNG lobbies, Rudd's early transition to an ETS was not enough to reverse the slide in competitiveness of Australia's fossil fuel mining industry.[196] Rather, to restore industrial competitiveness – and ensure that the billions of dollars of investment, thousands of jobs, and government revenue streams were preserved – Australia's carbon price would need to be abolished. As the APPEA's David Byers explained:

> The expected move to a floating price under the carbon pricing mechanism still represents an addition to the cost structure of Australian liquefied natural gas (LNG) exporters competing in global markets. It is important to recognise there is no international carbon price in operation. So while the move to a floating price may represent a short-term lowering of the price facing liable entities, Australia is still imposing a cost on its gas export industry that will not be borne by any of its LNG competitors. This will diminish its international competitive standing.[197]

The MCA's Mitch Hooke explained similarly:

> An early move to a floating carbon price based on the design elements of the existing carbon tax would not go far enough for the minerals industry. The current carbon pricing scheme should be scrapped immediately. Australia cannot afford to have a carbon pricing mechanism that puts Australian industry at a competitive disadvantage. The carbon tax distinctly disadvantages Australia's economy and an emissions trading scheme based on the foundations of the current policy will similarly impose unnecessary economic hardship relative to our export competitors.[198]

The opposition leader, Tony Abbott, was equally unimpressed with Rudd's policy change:

> The announcement today that the Government will bring forward planned changes to the carbon tax by one year is just a Kevin Rudd con job – fixed or floating, it is still a carbon tax. It will continue to be a tax on electricity bills which will hurt Australian families and hurt local businesses.... Labor can't be trusted on the carbon tax. Australians will now go to yet another election with the Labor leader

promising 'there will be no carbon tax under the government I lead'. Only the Coalition offers Australian families and businesses the certainty of no carbon tax.[199]

With the Federal Election looming, the APPEA launched 'a new multi-million dollar national campaign titled "Our Natural Advantage"'. The purpose of the campaign was to pressure the next government, whoever it was, to protect the competitive position of Australia's gas/LNG industry. As David Byers repeatedly explained in a series of media releases[200] in the lead up to the Election: '$150 billion worth of gas projects are currently being assessed by potential investors. If those resources are not developed Australia will lose jobs, cheaper energy, cleaner energy, and future tax revenues'. In terms of 'taxes and royalties', Byers continued, the oil and gas industry will potentially pay '$13 billion a year in by 2020 – that's the funding needs of about 25,000 public hospital beds, or enough to fund the annual education costs of one million students in government primary schools'. But this can only occur, Byers repeatedly concluded in the media releases: 'If our next Parliament – irrespective of who forms Government – addresses our sliding competitiveness before we lose the next wave of mega-projects to North America or East Africa'.

The MCA's pre-Election messages also set forth a reminder to both major political parties what was at stake if competitiveness was not restored:

> While the coal industry faces a more demanding environment – including from the world's biggest carbon tax – coal remains a powerful force for prosperity in our economy ... generating almost $50 billion a year in exports ... employs more than 180,000 people ... and adding at least $20 billion per annum to state and federal coffers in recent years.[201]

It is important to note that the coal lobby underwent two major changes in 2013. On 26 February 2013, the MCA announced that 2013 would be Mitch Hooke's last as leader. He had been CEO of the Council since 2002. And on 23 August 2013, the Australian Coal Association, along with its members, were subsumed into the Minerals Council of Australia. The ACA ceased to exist as a distinct entity.

The Federal Election was held on 7 September 2013. Up until this day, Rudd deployed the WW storyline to legitimise his ETS and the LL storyline to delegitimise Abbott's Direct Action scheme.[202] Rudd even adopted Abbott's vernacular: 'We're scrapping the tax'.[203] Abbott argued that only he could be trusted to abolish this 'toxic tax' and in doing so, restore prosperity to the country.

Conclusion

Chapter 3 examined Australian climate policy and diplomacy during the Gillard Labor Government (June 2010 to June 2013), and the short second period of the Rudd Labor Government (June to September 2013).

Julia Gillard's ascendency to Labor leader and Prime Minister in June 2010 demoted carbon pricing in importance (compared to Kevin Rudd), and signalled the start of the decline of the CNTA storyline to frame national climate policy (which had dominated during the Rudd years). In 2010 and 2011, a series of Critical Discourse Moments – namely, Gillard's replacement of Kevin Rudd in June 2010, the MPCCC announcement of September 2010, Gillard's 2011 agenda speech of November 2010, the price on carbon announcement of February 2011, and the Clean Energy Future announcement of July 2011 – failed to deploy the environmental CNTA storyline (rather deploying an increasingly narrow version of the economic CNTA storyline) to justify the establishment of a price on carbon. These series of missed opportunities to deploy the environmental CNTA storyline; combined with a sequential narrowing the economic CNTA storyline (perhaps as well as prematurely assuming storyline victory) significantly weakened the political potency of the CNTA story-line, and in doing so, as we shall see in Chapter 4, permitted the re-emergence of the CTA storyline, wielded by Tony Abbott, to a position of dominance in 2013. The MCA, the ACA, and the APPEA deployed the CTA storyline to delegitimise Gillard's carbon price.

Attempts to broaden out the economic CNTA storyline did occur throughout 2011. For example, in May 2011, two reports carried and cen-tralised the environmental CNTA storyline (Climate Council report; Garnaut report), and post-announcement, Gillard began to deploy strong versions of the environmental CNTA storyline, but her localised economic CNTA storyline still took priority.

Gillard also deployed the WW storyline to justify the establishment of a national price on carbon, and to legitimise the Clean Energy Act itself, which she described as in Australia's interests (i.e. the Act protects Aus-tralia's current and future interests – in other words: dirty and clean jobs). Over this same period, the fossil fuel lobby, initially deployed the WW, LL storyline binary to shape the carbon pricing mechanism so that each industry would receive maximum financial advantage under the scheme, but once legislated focused more on deploying the CTA storyline to dele-gitimise the Clean Energy Act as a whole. Despite industry conflict over the precise carbon price design, all lobbies overwhelmingly agreed that any national carbon price must be designed in a way that protected the competitiveness of Australian industry. The critical point to make here however, it that the final design of the Clean Energy Act, on the one hand, protected the competitiveness of Australia's existing fossil fuel industry (and the jobs and government revenue therein), and on the other hand, incentivised Australia's clean energy industry of the future – which is novel way to say that Australia's future competitive position compared to other countries relies on keeping up with the global transition towards low pollution economies ('Australia cannot be left behind', as Gillard explained).

Internationally, between 2010 and 2013, in a parallel timeframe to Labor's domestic negotiations over the Clean Energy Future design, which primarily took place in the MPCCC, Gillard and Combet sought to shape UNFCCC negotiations to protect Australia's industrial interests (and future low pollution industries). This was achieved by way of a two-pronged strategy. First, Combet encouraged the US and China, and Australia's trade competitors, to increase their commitment to the second period of the Kyoto process (2012–2020). This feature of Australian diplomacy culminated in Combet announcing at the COP17 in Durban the need for an 'environmentally effective outcome'. Second, Gillard and Combet built coalitions with Australia's traditional allies (the US and Commonwealth countries) and in its sphere of influence (New Zealand and Indonesia particularly) to encourage the UNFCCC Parties to agree to adopt REDD (and CCS to a lesser extent) under the Kyoto's CDM for industry offsetting purposes under the Clean Energy Act. The Australian Government also lobbies the UNFCCC directly, providing a series of submissions advocating for the inclusion of REDD and CCS activities.

Gillard believed that this diplomatic strategy would satisfy Australia's present and future economic interests, and to a lesser extent, Australia's environmental interests. In the first place, a 'environmentally effective' agreement would satisfy Australia's present industrial interests because the Clean Energy Future package was designed in such a way as to allocate liable entities 95 per cent of their permits for free, thus offsetting any potential competitive disadvantages arising from a national price on carbon. In the second place, if an 'environmentally effective' agreement could be struck, which Gillard and Combet argued required several essential 'building blocks' in place – namely, the inclusion of REDD+ activities under the CDM and the operationalisation of a global carbon market – then not only would Australia's immediate fossil fuel interests (and jobs) be protected, but so too would Australia's future economic interests – as well as Australia's environmental interests – as the world's major economies would be committed to developing lower pollution industries (and jobs) over time.

Gillard also sought to advance the interests of Australia's mining industry, and to a lesser extent the lower pollution industry, though a range of bilateral energy-based enterprises. She deployed the WW storyline to justify the sale of Australian uranium to Russia, and later to India (overturning Labor's long-standing opposition to Australian uranium exports). The government, the ACA and the MCA deployed the WW storyline to justify development and deployment of CCS technology, Gillard for example working with the US to commercialise this technology through the Australian-led Global Carbon Capture and Storage Institute. Further, in a series of bilateral meeting, the Prime Minister deployed the WW storyline to justify the continued sales of Australian LNG to Japan, Korea, and China. The APPEA deployed the WW storyline to justify these arrangements. In addition, she worked with the US, for example, to develop renewable energy technology partnerships. Government and industry overwhelming justified these energy-based solutions to climate change on the basis that they protected Australia's industrial interests.

Kevin Rudd returned to the Prime Ministership from June to September 2013. His central contribution to climate policy in this time was to bring forward the start date of the floating price from 2015 to 2014. Rudd and his climate minister, Mark Butler, deployed the WW storyline to justify this change, which significantly reduced the compliance costs on polluting industries. Rudd argued that this change would better protect industrial competitiveness. Despite this, the APPEA and the MCA deployed the LL storyline to delegitimise the scheme. Their central argument was that the change failed to restore the sliding competitiveness of Australia's mining industry, which, they argued had been diminishing since Gillard's pricing scheme commenced on 1 July 2012. The carbon price would have to be abolished to restore competitiveness (and ensure ongoing investment, jobs, and government revenue), they argued – something that the opposition leader, Tony Abbott, had fervently promised to do if elected in September 2013.

Ultimately, Chapter 3 revealed the existence of a 'master discourse' about protecting Australia's industrial competitiveness, shared between government and industry players, which shaped and constrained Australian climate policymaking at a national and international level. It also revealed the enabling influence of Labor's foreign policy 'ancillary discourse'. That is, Labor was driven in part by their sense of obligation to respond to the call of multilateralism and adopt domestic climate policy and multilateral climate norms (and in part by their agreement with the Green Party to strengthen their climate policies). This analysis permits a more sophisticated understanding of the factors that contract and expand Australia's domestic climate 'win-set' than Pearse's (and Putnam's) superficial veto players understanding, which in addition, can only explain policy continuity.

Notes

1 Anabela Carvalho, 'Representing the Politics of the Greenhouse Effect: Discursive Strategies in the British Media', *Critical Discourse Studies*, vol. 2, no. 1 (2005), p. 6.
2 Julia Gillard, Speech, House of Representatives, 24 June 2010.
3 Tony Abbott, Speech, House of Representatives, 24 June 2010.
4 Julia Gillard, Press Conference, 24 June 2010. See also Julia Gillard: 'Interview with Kerry O'Brien', The 730 Report, ABC TV, 24 June 2010; 'Interview with Laurie Oaks, Weekend Today', Channel 9, 27 June 2010; 'Interview with Jon Faine', 774 ABC Radio, 29 June 2010.
5 Julia Gillard, 'Press Conference', 24 June 2010.
6 Benjamin Parr, *Australian Climate Policy and Diplomacy: The Transition Years, John Howard to Kevin Rudd*, PhD Thesis, University of Melbourne 2015.
7 Julia Gillard, Speech, 'Moving Forward Together on Climate Change', University of Queensland, 23 July 2010. See also, Julia Gillard, Penny Wong, and Wayne Swan, Media Releases, 25 July 2010: 'Tax Breaks for Green Buildings'; 'Cleaner Car Rebate to Scrap Inefficient Cars'; 'New Emission Standards for Cars'; 'Building Consensus in the Community'; 'Connecting Renewable Energy to Australian Homes'; 'Tougher Emissions Standards for New Coal Fired Power Stations'; 'Reward for Early Action'. See also, Julia Gillard: 'Interview with Alan Jones', 2GB, 27 July 2010; 'Doorstop Interview', Melbourne, 29 July 2010.
8 Julia Gillard, Speech, 'Moving Forward Together on Climate Change', University of Queensland, 23 July 2010.
9 Julia Gillard, 'Interview with Lisa Wilkinson', Channel 9, 2 August 2010.
10 See for example, 'Claims Gillard Opposed Paid Parental Leave', ABC News, 27 July 2010; 'Julia Gillard Admits Early Doubts on Pension Rise and Paid Parental Leave Scheme', The Australian, 28 July 2010. See also, 'Kevin Rudd Admits to Leaking Against Julia Gillard', Financial Review, 22 June 2015.
11 Julia Gillard, 'Interview with Kerry O'Brian', 730 Report, 3 August 2010. See also Julia Gillard: 'Interview', ABC Sydney, 2 August 2010; 'Interview with Fran Kelly', ABC National, 4 August 2010; 'Interview with Jon Faine', ABC 774, 6 August 2010; 'Interview with Laurie Oaks', Channel 9, 15 August 2010.
12 See for example, Julia Gillard, 'The Choice for Australians', National Press Club Address, 19 August 2010.
13 Julia Gillard, Speech, 'ALP Campaign Launch', Brisbane, 16 August 2010.
14 This interview cannot be found on the Prime Minister's archived website or The Labor Party's website. Rather, see 'Julia Gillard Did Not Lie About Carbon Tax (There is No Carbon Tax in Australia)', YouTube clip: www.youtube.com/watch?v=-EyW7oFk6n8
15 Julia Gillard, 'Interview with Lyndal Curtis', ABC AM, 20 August 2010. See also 'Julia Gillard's Carbon Price Promise', The Australian, 20 August 2010.
16 Julia Gillard and Wayne Swan, 'Press Conference', 11 September 2010.
17 See for example, 'Greens Opposition to Gas and LNG is Counter-Intuitive', APPEA, Media Release, 27 October 2010; Mitch Hooke, 'CEO's Review', MCA, Annual Report, 2010, p. 11.
18 Ralph Hillman, ACA, Media Releases: 'Carbon Capture and Storage is Essential to Reduce Global Emissions', 20 July 2010; 'Carbon Capture and Storage: A Key Technology for Australia's Clean Energy Future', 23 July 2010.

19 Belinda Robinson, 'Oil and Gas Industry Welcomes New Government', APPEA, Media Release, 7 September 2010.

20 Ralph Hillman, 'Carbon Capture and Storage: A Key Technology for Australia's Clean Energy Future', Media Release, ACA, 23 July 2010.

21 Mitch Hooke, 'Statement', MCA, 24 June 2010.

22 Julia Gillard, Press Conference, Canberra, 16 September 2010.

23 Tony Abbott, 'Doorstop Interview', Adelaide, 17 September 2010.

24 Julia Gillard, 'Interview with Paul Bongiorno', 26 September 2010.

25 Julia Gillard, Wayne Swan, Greg Combet, Bob Brown, Christine Milne, 'Joint Press Conference', Canberra, 27 September 2010.

26 Julia Gillard, 'Speech to the Australian Industry Group', Canberra, 26 October 2010.

27 Julia Gillard, 'Press Conference', Newcastle, 8 October 2010.

28 Julia Gillard, 'Press Conference', Barrow Island, 9 October 2010.

29 Julia Gillard, 'New Funding for Institute to Support Carbon Capturing Efforts in Developing Nations', 9 October 2010.

30 Julia Gillard, 'US and Australia Join Forces on Solar Power', 7 November 2010.

31 Julia Gillard: 'Indonesia-Australia Joint Statement', Media Release, 2 November 2010; 'A Joint Announcement on the Commencement of Negotiations on an Indonesia-Australia Economic Partnership', Jakarta, Indonesia, 2 November 2010.

32 Julia Gillard, 'Entry into force of the Australia-Russia Nuclear Cooperation Agreement', Seoul, Korea, 11 November 2010.

33 Julia Gillard, 'Press Conference', Yokohama, Japan, 14 November 2010.

34 'APEC 2010 Leaders' Declaration', Yokohama, Japan, 13 November 2010.

35 Julia Gillard, '2011 Will be a Year of Delivery and Decision: Speech to the Committee for the Economic Development of Australia', Sydney, 29 November 2010.

36 Mitch Hooke, MCA, Annual Report, December 2010.

37 Ralph Hillman, 'Development of Carbon Capture and Storage Technology in Queensland', ACA, Media Release, 19 December 2010.

38 'Climate Change Policy Position: A Government–Industry Partnership for a Clean Energy Future', APPEA, November 2010. See also 'Natural Gas Industry Welcomes Climate Change Committee', APPEA, Media Release, 27 September 2010.

39 Greg Combet, 'Australian Delegation to Cancun', Media Release, 29 November 2010. See also, Greg Combet, 'Outcome at Cancun', Media Release, 11 December 2010.

40 Greg Combet, 'Strengthening Australia's Climate Change Partnership with Indonesia', Media Release, 9 December 2010.

41 See for example, 'Warm Praise for Cancun Deal to Stop Logging', ABC News, 16 December 2010.

42 Greg Combet, 'Australia Climate Finance -Australia Joins Partnership for Carbon Market Readiness', Media Release, 10 December 2010.

43 Julia Gillard, 'Press Conference', Canberra, 7 December 2010.

44 Julia Gillard, 'Interview with Alex Kirk', ABC AM, 28 January 2011.

45 'Coal Miners to Blame for Queensland Floods, says Australian Greens Leader Bob Brown', News.com.au, 16 January 2011.

46 Julia Gillard, 'I See What Needs to be Done and I Will Do It: Speech to the National Press Club', 27 January 2011.

47 Julia Gillard, 'Transcript of Interview with Paul Bongiorno', Meet the Press, Channel 10, 6 February 2011.
48 See for example, Julia Gillard, 'Transcript of Press Conference', Canberra, 7 February 2011.
49 Julia Gillard, 'Interview with Paul Bongiorno', 6 February 2011.
50 Julia Gillard, Greg Combet, 'Climate Change Framework Announced – Transcript of Joint Press Conference', Canberra, 24 February 2011. See also Julia Gillard, 'Climate Change Framework Announced', Media Release, 24 February 2011.
51 Julia Gillard, 'Transcript of Interview with Heather Ewart', the 7.30 Report, 24 February 2011.
52 See for example, Julia Gillard, 'Transcript of Interview with Laurie Oakes', Today Show, Channel 9, 27 February 2011. See also, Julia Gillard, 'Transcript of Interview with John Laws', 2SM, 28 February 2011.
53 See for example, Julia Gillard, 'Transcript of Interview with Neil Mitchell', 3AW, 25 February 2011.
54 Ralph Hillman, 'Coal Industry Competitiveness at Risk from Carbon Tax', ACA, Media Release, March 2011.
55 Ralph Hillman, 'Coal Industry Competitiveness at Risk from Carbon Tax', ACA, Media Release, March 2011.
56 Mitch Hooke, 'International Action on Carbon Pricing: An Update', MCA, Briefing Note No1, March 2011.
57 Belinda Robinson, 'Garnaut Paper on Carbon Pricing Reinforces Role of Gas Industry', APPEA, Media Release, 17 March 2011.
58 Julia Gillard, 'Interview', ABC, 730 Report, 8 March. See also, Julia Gillard, 'Press Conference', Washington, March 2011.
59 Julia Gillard: 'Interview', ABC, 730 Report, 8 March; 'Press Conference', Washington, March 2011; 'Press Conference with Senator McCain', 8 March 2011. See also, Julia Gillard: 'Address to the Congress of the United States', Washington, 8 March 2011; 'Press Conference', New York, 10 March 2011; 'Interview with Erin Burnett', CNBC, 10 March 2011.
60 Julia Gillard, 'Trans-Tasman Business Circle Luncheon', Auckland, 15 February 2011.
61 Julia Gillard, 'Australia-Mongolia Joint Statement', 23 February 2011.
62 Julia Gillard, 'Making a Difference for The Small and Medium Countries of The World', Speech to the African Union Permanent Representatives, New York, 10 March 2011.
63 Julia Gillard, 'Doorstop Interview', Canberra, 21 March 2011. See also, Julia Gillard, 'Speech to the Inaugural Whitlam Institute Gough Whitlam Oration', Sydney, 31 March 2011.
64 Julia Gillard, 'Interview with David Speers', Sky News, 19 April 2011.
65 Mitch Hooke, 'Europe's Carbon Pricing Scheme Protects Exports, Australia's CPRS Does Not', MCA, Media Release, 6 April 2011.
66 Mitch Hooke, 'Minerals Sector Welcomes Trade Policy Statement', MCA, Media Release, 12 April 2011.
67 Belinda Robinson, 'LNG Greenhouse benefit Confirmed by New Study', APPEA, Media Release, 10 April 2011.
68 See for example, Julia Gillard: 'Question and Answer Session Following Speech to the Japan National Press Club', Tokyo, 22 April 2011; 'Press Conference', Seoul, 25 April 2011; 'Doorstop Interview', Beijing, 27 April 2011.

69 Julia Gillard, 'Joint Press Conference', Gladstone, 27 May 2011.
70 'The Critical Decade: Climate Science, Risks and Responses', Climate Commission, Commonwealth of Australia, May 2011.
71 Julia Gillard, 'Joint Doorstop Interview', Canberra, 23 May 2011.
72 'Carbon Emission Policies in Key Economies', Productivity Commission, Research Report, Commonwealth of Australia, May 2011.
73 Julia Gillard, 'Joint Press Conference', Canberra, 15 June 2011.
74 'Proposed Architecture and Implementation Arrangements for a Carbon Pricing Mechanism', APPEA, Submission, May 2011, p. i.
75 'Proposed Architecture and Implementation Arrangements for a Carbon Pricing Mechanism', APPEA, Submission, May 2011, p. 9.
76 'A New Carbon Pricing Scheme', MCA, Submission, May 2011.
77 For example, 'Coal Industry Competitiveness at Risk from Carbon Tax', ACA, Media Release, 3 March 2011.
78 'A New Carbon Pricing Scheme', MCA, Submission, May 2011, p. 35.
79 'A New Carbon Pricing Scheme', MCA, Submission, May 2011. See also Mitch Hooke, 'Global Developments on Climate Change Undermines Carbon Tax Argument', MCA, Media Release, 30 May 2011; 'Minerals Council of Australia: Budget 2011', MCA, Media Release, 10 May 2011.
80 'Carbon Tax Proposal', ACA, Submission, 11 May 2011. See also, 'Coal Industry Submission Provides Opportunity for a Carbon Tax Circuit Breaker', ACA, Media Release, 13 May 2011.
81 'Proposed Architecture and Implementation Arrangements for a Carbon Pricing Mechanism', APPEA, Submission, May 2011.
82 Julia Gillard: 'Australia Not Alone on Climate Change Action', Media Release, 14 June 2011; 'Joint Press Conference', 15 June 2011.
83 Julia Gillard: 'Kakadu Vulnerable to Climate Change Impacts', Media Release, 2 June 2011; 'Joint Press Conference', 2 June 2011.
84 Julia Gillard, 'Interview with David Koch', Sunrise, Channel 7, 27 June 2011.
85 Julia Gillard, 'Doorstop Interview', Perth, 25 June 2011.
86 'Australian Coal's Competitors Face no Carbon Tax on Fugitive Emissions', ACA, Media Release, 8 June 2011.
87 'Carbon Tax Impact Could Close Coal Mines Within Three Years', ACA, Media Release, 14 June 2011.
88 'Australian Coal's Competitors Face no Carbon Tax on Fugitive Emissions', ACA, Media Release, 8 June 2011. See also 'Carbon Tax Impact Could Close Coal Mines Within Three Years', ACA, Media Release, 14 June 2011; Ralph Hillman, 'How the Government's Carbon Tax Will Impact the Australian Coal Industry and Diminish Economic Growth', National Press Club Address, Canberra, 6 July 2011; 'How the Government's Carbon Tax Will Impact the Australian Coal Industry and Diminish Economic Growth', ACA, Media Release, 6 July 2011.
89 'Australian Coal's Competitors Face no Carbon Tax on Fugitive Emissions', ACA, Media Release, 8 June 2011.
90 Julia Gillard, 'Interview with Jon Faine', ABC 774, 27 June 2011.
91 Julia Gillard, 'Government to Announce Price on Pollution', Media Release, 4 July 2011. See also Julia Gillard, 'Press Conference', 4 July 2011.
92 'Securing a Clean Energy Future: The Australian Government's Climate Change Plan', Commonwealth of Australia, July 2011.

93 'Securing a Clean Energy Future: The Australian Government's Climate Change Plan', Commonwealth of Australia, July 2011.

94 Julia Gillard, 'Joint Press Conference', 10 July 2011. See also Julia Gillard, 'Putting a Price on Carbon Pollution', Media Release, 10 July 2011.

95 Julia Gillard, 'Address to the Nation', 10 July 2011.

96 Julia Gillard, 'Assistance for Nine Out of Ten Australian Households', Media Release, 10 July 2011.

97 Julia Gillard, 'Extra Support for Pensioners and Self-funded Retirees', Media Release, 10 July 2011.

98 Julia Gillard, 'Address to the Nation', 10 July 2011.

99 Julia Gillard, 'Address to the Nation', 10 July 2011.

100 Julia Gillard, '$300 Million for Steel Support Under Carbon Price Plan', Media Release, 10 July 2011.

101 Julia Gillard, '$300 Million for Steel Support Under Carbon Price Plan', Media Release, 10 July 2011.

102 Julia Gillard, 'Support for Australia's Coal Sector', 10 July 2011.

103 Julia Gillard, 'Transforming Australia's Electricity Generation Sector', Media Release, 10 July 2011.

104 Julia Gillard, 'Securing a Clean Energy Future for Australia', Media Release, 10 July 2011.

105 Julia Gillard, 'Government Supports Innovation and Renewable Energy', Media Release, 10 July 2011.

106 Ralph Hillman, 'Carbon Tax to Constrain Growth and Cost Jobs', ACA, Media Release, 10 July 2011. See also, Ralph Hillman, 'Carbon Tax will Punish Jobs and Investment in Coal Industry', ACA, Media Release, 12 July 2011.

107 Mitch Hooke, 'Carbon Tax Package', MCA, Media Release, 10 July 2011.

108 '2009 Re-Run Will Not Reduce Emissions Where Most Needed', APPEA, Media Release, 10 July 2011.

109 'Coal Campaign to Highlight Regional Impact of Carbon Tax' ACA, Media Release, 18 July 2011.

110 For example, Julia Gillard: 'Interview with Aaron Kearney', ABC Newcastle, 19 July 2011; 'Visit to Centennial Coal's Mandalong Mine', 19 July 2011; 'Doorstop Interview', La Trobe Valley, 16 July 2011; 'Interview with Chris Coleman', ABC Riverina, 20 July 2011; 'Doorstop Interview', Gurrandah, 20 July 2011; 'Doorstop Interview', Moorooka, 21 July 2011; 'Joint Doorstop Interview', Townsville, 22 July 201; 'Press Conference', Hobart, 23 July 2011; 'Ground-breaking Solar Energy Project Announced in Queensland', 13 April 2011.

111 Julia Gillard, 'Strong Growth, Low Pollution Under a Carbon Price', Media Release, 10 July 2011.

112 Julia Gillard, 'A Great Clean Energy Future, A Great Reform Agenda', Address to the National Press Club, 14 July 2011.

113 'Coal Campaign to Highlight Regional Impact of Carbon Tax', ACA, Media Release, 18 July 2011.

114 'Carbon Tax Coal Jobs Impact Real', ACA, Media Statement, 30 August 2011.

115 'Carbon Tax to Hit Queensland Coal Communities', ACA, Media Release, 21 July 2011.

116 Mitch Hooke, 'Australian Trade and Industry Alliance Carbon Tax Advertising', Media Release, 21 July 2011. The ATI Alliance included, the

Australian Chamber of Commerce and Industry, Australian Coal Association, Australian Retailers Association, Housing Industry Association, Manufacturing Australia and the Minerals Council of Australia.

117 'Australian Trade and Industry Alliance Carbon Tax Advertising', Media Release, 21 July 2011

118 'Minerals Industry to Pay A Record $23.4 Billion In Taxes + Royalties: 2010–11', Media Release, 2 August 2011.

119 Julia Gillard, 'Joint Press Conference', Canberra, 3 September 2011.

120 Julia Gillard, 'Joint Statement with the President of the European Commission', 5 September 2011.

121 Julia Gillard, 'Joint Press Conference with Prime Minister John Key', Auckland, 7 September 2011.

122 Julia Gillard, 'Introduction of the Clean Energy Bill 2011', Canberra, 13 September 2011.

123 'Government's Hollow Words Leave 950,000 Manufacturing Workers Fully Exposed to World's Biggest Carbon Tax', MCA, September 2011.

124 'Briefing note: How the Carbon Pricing Scheme Risks Manufacturing Jobs', Australian Trade and Industry Alliance, Briefing Note, September 2011

125 'Full Impact of Carbon Tax on Coal Revealed', ACA, Media Release, 10 October 2011.

126 'Submission to the Joint Select Committee on Australia's Clean Energy Future Legislation Inquiry into the Clean Energy Future Legislative Package', ACA, Submission, September 2011. See also, 'Carbon Tax Hits Coal Jobs at The Worst Possible Time', ACA, Media Release, 27 September 2011. 'Joint Select Committee on Australia's Clean Energy Future Legislation', APPEA, Submission, September 2011.

127 'Submission Under the Cancun Agreements Modalities and Procedures for Carbon Dioxide Capture and Storage in Geological Formations as Clean Development Mechanism Project Activities', Australia Government, February 2011.

128 'Joint Submission Under the Cancun Agreements, Reducing Emissions from Deforestation and Forest Degradation in Developing Countries', Australian Government and Indonesian Government, December 2011.

129 'Submission under the Cancun Agreements, Reducing Emissions from Deforestation and Forest Degradation in Developing Countries', Australian Government, Submission to the UNFCCC, September 2011.

130 'Submission Under the Cancun Agreements, Enhanced Action on Mitigation and Measurement, Reporting and Verification', Australian Government, Submission to the UNFCCC, March 2011; 'Submission under the Cancún Agreements Enhanced Action on Measurement, Reporting and Verification', Australian Government, Submission to the UNFCCC, September 2011.

131 Mitch Hooke, 'Passage of The Carbon Tax Through the House of Representatives', MCA, Media Release, 12 October 2011.

132 'Coal Remains Committed to Fixing Carbon Tax Flaws', ACA, Media Release, 12 October 2011.

133 Julia Gillard, 'Joint Press Conference', Canberra, 8 November 2011.

134 'Passing of Carbon Tax Legislation', ACA, Statement, 8 November 2011.

135 Mitch Hooke, 'Passage of The Carbon Tax Legislation', MCA, Media Release, 8 November 2011.

136 Julia Gillard: 'Joint Press Conference with Commonwealth Secretary-General Sharma', 30 October 2011; 'Joint Statement of the Prime Ministers of Trinidad and Tobago and the Commonwealth of Australia', 25 October 2011.

137 Julia Gillard, 'Press Conference', Cannes, 4 November 2011.

138 Julia Gillard, 'Press Conference', Honolulu, 11 November 2011.

139 '1st Indonesia-Australia Annual Leaders' Meeting', Joint Communique, 20 November 2011.

140 Greg Combet, 'Durban and Beyond: Building a Comprehensive Climate Change Regime', Speech, 25 November 2011.

141 See for example, Greg Combet, 'UN Climate Change Conference 2011', ABC PM, 2 December 2011. See also Greg Combet: 'UN Climate Change Conference 2011 in Durban, South Africa', ABC, 6 December 2011; 'UN Climate Change Conference 2011 in Durban, South Africa', Sky News, 8 December 2011.

142 Greg Combet, 'UN Climate Change Conference 2011', ABC PM, 2 December 2011.

143 Greg Combet, 'Durban, South Africa – Interview with Sabra Lane', ABC Radio, 12 December 2011.

144 Greg Combet, 'Breakthrough at Durban Climate Change Conference', Media Release, 11 December 2011.

145 Julia Gillard, 'Press Conference', Canberra, 12 December 2011.

146 Julia Gillard, 'Interview with Mark Parton', 2CC, 3 February 2012.

147 Julia Gillard, 'Press Conference', Canberra, 27 February 2012.

148 Julia Gillard, 'Press Conference', Melbourne, 24 February 2012.

149 Julia Gillard, 'Joint Doorstop Interview', Melbourne, 30 June 2012.

150 Julia Gillard, 'Press Conference', Parramatta, 3 April 2012.

151 Julia Gillard, 'Joint Statement with the Prime Minister of New Zealand', 29 January 2012.

152 Julia Gillard, 'Joint Press Conference', Rio de Janeiro, 20 June 2012.

153 Julia Gillard, 'Brazil-Australia Strategic Partnership', Media Release, 21 June 2012.

154 'The Future We Want', Outcome Document of the United Nations Conference on Sustainable Development, Rio de Janeiro, Brazil, 20–22 June 2012.

155 Julia Gillard, 'Australia's Clean Energy Future', Media Release, 1 July 2012.

156 David Byers, 'Carbon Pricing Mechanism to add Cost to LNG Exporters', APPEA, Media Release, 1 July 2012.

157 Mitch Hooke, 'The Carbon and Mining Taxes', MCA, Statement, 1 July 2012.

158 Julia Gillard, 'Joint Doorstop Interview', Melbourne, 1 July 2012.

159 For example, Julia Gillard: 'Interview with John Laws', 2SM, 2 July 2012; Interview with Leigh Sales', 7.30 ABC, 25 July 2012; 'Interview with Sarbra Lane', ABC AM, 8 August 2012.

160 Julia Gillard, 'Interview with Paul Bongiorno, Rafael Epstein and Patricia Karvelas', Meet the Press, Channel 10, 2 December 2012.

161 Julia Gillard, 'Interview with Leon Byner', 5AA, 3 December 2012.

162 Julia Gillard: 'COAG Reaches Agreement On Electricity Market Reform' Media Release, 7 December 2012; 'COAG Joint Press Conference', 7 December 2012.

163 Julia Gillard, Doorstop Interview from Rarotonga', Cook Islands, 28 August 2012.

164 Julia Gillard, 'Practical Progress Towards Realising Those Ideals in The World', Speech to the United Nations General Assembly, New York, 26 September 2012.

165 Julia Gillard, 'Address to the 50th Anniversary Australia Japan Foundation Joint Business Conference', Sydney, 8 October 2012.

166 Julia Gillard, 'Press Conference', New Delhi, India, 17 October 2012. See also, Julia Gillard: 'Doorstop Interview', New Delhi, 16 October 2012; 'Press Conference', New Delhi, India, 15 October 2012; 'Australia and India: Old Friends, New Partners', Speech to Indian Business Chambers Lunch, New Delhi, India, 17 October 2012; 'Doorstop Interview', New Delhi, 17 October 2012.

167 Julia Gillard, 'Joint Statement – Prime Minister of Australia and Prime Minister of India', New Delhi, India, 17 October 2012.

168 'Alternative Approaches to Addressing Non-Permanence Under the Clean Development Mechanism', Australian Government, Submission to the UNFCCC, September 2012.

169 'Submission Under the Kyoto Protocol: Quantified Emission Limitation or Reduction Objective', Australia Government, Submission to the UNFCCC, November 2012.

170 Greg Combet, 'Australia Joins Kyoto Protocol Second Commitment as World on Track to 2015 Climate Change Agreement', Joint Media Release, 9 December 2012.

171 'State of the Industry', APPEA, Report, November 2012, p. 13. See also, 'Policy Inaction Threatens Gas Industry Investment, National Prosperity', APPEA, Media Release, 30 November 2012.

172 'Advancing Australia', APPEA and Deloitte, June 2012; 'Summary of Advancing Australia', APPEA and Deloitte, June 2012; 'Advancing Australia – Supplementary Analysis', APPEA and Deloitte, November 2012.

173 Mitch Hooke, 'Regaining our Competitiveness', MCA, Statement, 17 September 2012. 'Opportunity at Risk: Regaining our Competitive Edge in Minerals Resources', MCA and Port Jackson Partners, Report, September 2012.

174 Julia Gillard, 'Interview with Charlie Pickering, Gorgi Coghlan, Natasha Exelby and James Mathison', The Project, Channel 10, 17 January 2013.

175 On 4 August, Kevin Rudd announced that the election would take place on 7 September 2013.

176 Tony Abbott, 'Statement', Parliament House, Canberra, 30 January 2013.

177 See for example, Tony Abbott: 'Hope Reward Opportunity', Address to the National Press Club of Australia, Canberra, 31 January 2013; 'Committee for Economic Development of Australia State of the Nation Address', Sydney 15 February 2013; 'Matter of Public Importance', House of Representatives, Parliament House, 20 March 2013.

178 Julia Gillard, 'Doorstop Interview', 18 February 2013.

179 Julia Gillard, 'Address to the National Press Club', 30 January 2013; Julia Gillard, 'Interview with Karl Stefanovic', Today, Channel 9, 31 January 2013.

180 Julia Gillard, 'Interview with Geoff Hutchison', ABC Perth, 13 June 2013.

181 'EU Carbon Price Crashes to Record Low', *The Guardian*, 25 January 2013.

182 Julia Gillard: 'Interview with David Speers', Sky News, 15 May 2013; 'Interview With Sabra Lane', ABC News, 15 May 2013.

183 Julia Gillard, 'Interview with David Speers', Sky News, 26 June 2013.
184 Julia Gillard, Final Speech as Prime Minister. To view this speech, and the day's events, see Michelle Grattan, 'Blog on ALP Leadership Spill', 26 June 2013.
185 Kevin Rudd, 'Press Conference', Canberra, 28 June 2013. See also, Kevin Rudd, 'National Press Club Address Q&A', 11 July 2013.
186 Kevin Rudd, 'Press Conference', Newcastle, 1 July 2013.
187 Kevin Rudd, 'Press Conference', Newcastle, 1 July 2013.
188 Kevin Rudd, 'Transcript of Doorstop Interview', Cairns, 14 July 2013.
189 Kevin Rudd, 'Transcript of Doorstop Interview', Cairns, 14 July 2013.
190 Kevin Rudd, Wayne Swan, and Mark Butler, 'Joint Press Conference', Townsville, 16 July 2013.
191 Kevin Rudd, Wayne Swan, and Mark Butler, 'Joint Press Conference', Townsville, 16 July 2013.
192 Kevin Rudd, 'Joint Doorstop Interview', Gladstone, 17 July 2013.
193 Kevin Rudd, Wayne Swan, and Mark Butler, 'Joint Press Conference', Townsville, 16 July 2013.
194 Kevin Rudd, Wayne Swan, and Mark Butler, 'Joint Press Conference', Townsville, 16 July 2013.
195 Kevin Rudd, Wayne Swan, and Mark Butler, 'Joint Press Conference', Townsville, 16 July 2013.
196 'Australia has to Again be Cost-Competitive', APPEA, Media Release, 26 May 2013.
197 David Byers, 'Carbon Pricing Mechanism Changes: Cost Competitiveness Issues Remain', APPEA, Media Release, 14 July 2013.
198 Mitch Hooke, 'Redesign Carbon Pricing Scheme – Don't Just Tinker with It', MCA, Statement, 12 July 2013.
199 Tony Abbott: 'Kevin Rudd's Carbon Con', Media Release, 14 July 2013; 'Kevin Rudd Misleads Australian Families on The Costs of His Carbon Tax', Media Release, 16 July 2013.
200 See for example, 'Australia has to Again be Cost-Competitive', APPEA, Media Release, 26 May 2013; 'Natural Gas is Australia's Natural Advantage – Campaign Launch', APPEA, Media Release, 29 July 2013; 'Election 2013', APPEA, Media Release, 4 August 2013.
201 Mitch Hooke, 'New Mine a Vote of Confidence in The Future of Australian Coal Sector', MCA, Statement, 4 September 2013.
202 See for example, Kevin Rudd: 'Doorstop Interview', Mackay, 17 July 2013; 'Doorstop Interview', Balmain, 22 July 2013; 'Doorstop Interview', Melbourne, 24 July 2013; 'Interview with Andrew Bolt', Perth, 28 July 2013.
203 Kevin Rudd, 'Doorstop Interview', Melbourne, 24 July 2013.

4   The Abbott Coalition Government

Introduction

Chapter 4 explores Australian climate policy and diplomacy in the period from September 2013 to September 2015, covering the Abbott Coalition Government.

This chapter reveals the key discourses that shaped and legitimated climate policy and diplomacy for the Abbott Government and the Australian fossil fuel lobby – the Australian Coal Association (ACA), the Minerals Council of Australia (MCA) and Australian Petroleum Production and Exploration Association (APPEA). It shows that key government actors, principally Prime Minister Tony Abbott and his environment minister, Greg Hunt, and key fossil fuel lobbyists, principally, chief executives, Mitch Hooke, then Brendan Pearson (MCA), and David Byers, then Malcolm Roberts (APPEA) shared a 'master discourse' about industrial competitiveness which dominated the meaning of the national interest, and served to make some domestic climate and energy policies and international positions and diplomatic missions seem natural and necessary, while excluding others. Again, similarly to the previous chapter, this indicates that an 'invisible' hegemonic domestic discourse – qua social structure – effectively served to veto certain policy options, which is consistent with Gramsci's notion of an 'historic bloc', and quite apart from prioritising the agency of certain actors according to Pearse's thesis (and Putnam's understanding of the 'win-set').

This chapter also reveals the existence of an 'ancillary discourse' about Liberal-Coalition Party foreign policy traditions, which can help explain variation in climate diplomacy between the major political parties. This discourse directed the Abbott Government's climate diplomacy away from multilateral initiatives and cooperation, and towards bilateral and plurilateral initiatives among like-minded parties. Indeed, this discourse permitted Tony Abbott to build coalitions abroad in energy and climate change that served to not only protect, but advance, the competitive position of Australia's fossil fuel industry with relative impunity towards the multilateral climate effort. This chapter also continues to investigate the role that storylines play in legitimising policies. Again, similarly to Chapter 3, it explores the role of the cost-to-act (CTA) versus the cost-not-to-act (CNTA) storylines; and the lose–lose (LL) versus the win–win (WW) storylines. The chapter shows that Prime Minister Abbott and the key fossil fuel lobbyists deployed the CTA storyline to justify their opposition to the Clean Energy Act 2011, which manifested in their shared support for its immediate abolishment. This storyline expresses the view that Australia's Clean Energy Act 2011 had compromised Australia's and the fossil fuel industry's international competitiveness, and would continue to do so, and would therefore 'cost' jobs, investment, and government revenue. As we shall see, Abbott deployed the CTA storyline to justify abolishing it long after the fact to support his incumbency as Prime Minister, as well as many other political events related to taxation, the economy, elections, among others.

The opposing storyline, the CNTA storyline, did not appear in government or industry texts in the Abbott years. In the Gillard years, as we saw, this storyline expressed the view that avoiding, or delaying, the introduction of a national carbon pricing mechanism would only serve to increase the economic – and environmental, expressed sparingly – 'costs' over time (i.e. unless Australia acts it will cost future low pollution jobs). However, a series of missed opportunities, and the sequential narrowing of this storyline, helped facilitate the re-emergence of the CTA storyline. As Chapter 4 shows, Abbott's election victory in September 2013 served to replace the CNTA storyline with the CTA storyline as the dominant frame of reference for establishing a national-wide carbon pricing mechanism. It also shows that throughout the Abbott years, five more Critical Discourse Moments occurred whereby Abbott and industry sought to entrench (via the process of abolishing the Clean Energy Act) and then institutionalise (via the process of legislating the government's centrepiece climate policy, the Emissions Reduction Fund (ERF)) the CTA storyline in Australian climate policy and diplomacy – that is, the ERF became a legal manifestation of the shared government and industry view that pricing carbon is an unwelcome economic 'cost' on Australian industry and Australians.

The second set of storylines WW, LL, were deployed either to delegitimise carbon pricing versus legitimise the ERF and Australia's accompanying post-2020 emission reduction target; or to justify an energy-based solution to climate change (i.e. uranium exports). This chapter reveals that the government and the fossil fuel industry regularly deployed the LL storyline to justify (and delegitimise) the abolition of the Clean Energy Act 2011. However, while the government deployed the WW storyline to legitimise the ERF policy, industry actors deployed the WW, LL storyline to justify certain ERF designs. So, again, we see industry not simply rejecting the policy outright, rather seeking to shape it to serve the interests of their respective corporate members.

The chapter begins in September 2013, in the aftermath of Labor's electoral loss to the Coalition Party, led by vocal climate science sceptic, Tony Abbott.

* * *

The Federal Election of 7 September 2013 was over. The Labor Party, led by Kevin Rudd (after replacing Julia Gillard in its lead up), had been convincingly defeated. The Liberal/National Coalition Party, led by Tony Abbott, had won 90 seats in the House of Representatives, with Labor only managing 55 seats. The Greens, Katter's Australian Party, and the Palmer United Party (PUP), had won one seat each, and two Independents made up the 150-seat chamber. The composition of the 76-person Senate included 17 Coalition senators, 12 Labor, 4 Greens, 2 PUP, and 5 senators from minor parties. Complex preference deals led to the most crossbench senators in Australia's history.

Despite this, Tony Abbott was resolute: 'I do expect the Parliament to respect the Government's mandate, and at the heart of that mandate is repealing the carbon tax'.[1] New senators would take their place on 1 July 2014. This meant that if Abbott wanted to abolish the Clean Energy Act prior to this date, he would need to work with the existing Senate, which meant convincing the Labor Party to 'scrap the tax'. To help achieve this, Abbott repeatedly deployed the CTA storyline to justify Labor parliamentarians – particularly senators, and their core constituents, workers unions – supporting the repeal of Labor's carbon price. For example:

> If the Labor Party still wants to be the party of the worker, surely it's going to have to respect measures that are going to make it easier for the workers of Australia to have a job and to keep a job and the trouble with the carbon tax is that it's a handbrake on growth, investment and employment.[2]

Abbott's election victory can be understood as the first Critical Discourse Movement of his Prime Ministership, and one that signalled that the CTA storyline had replaced Labor's (economic) CNTA storyline as the dominant frame in which to conceive national climate policy.

The Abbott Coalition Government was sworn-in on 18 September 2013, Tony Abbott becoming the 28th Prime Minister of Australia. 'We are determined to honour our commitment to scrap the carbon tax', Abbott declared, quite unusually, at the swearing-in ceremony.[3] He then announced his new ministry. Greg Hunt would be appointed Minister for the Environment, 'with the responsibility for the abolition of the carbon tax and implementation of the Coalition's Direct Action plan', the Prime Minister declared.[4] Not wasting any time, the following day Hunt phoned the chief climate commissioner, Professor Tim Flannery, to tell him to shut down the Climate Commission, which was established in February 2011 and charged with providing public information about climate impacts and solutions.[5]

Australia's gas/LNG and coal lobbies welcomed the Abbott Government with similar messages: that the carbon price had damaged their industrial competitiveness and it was now time to restore their competitiveness by abolishing it. For example, the chief of the Australian Petroleum and Production Exploration Association (APPEA), David Byers, asserted:

> The APPEA looks forward to working with the Government to maintain our industry's continued growth and to address the major challenge of Australia's sliding global competitiveness. A high-cost local environment and the emergence of new LNG competitors in East Africa, North America and elsewhere are making it much harder to win market share and attract investment.[6]

Similarly, the chief of the Minerals Council of Australia (MCA), Mitch Hooke asserted:

> The minerals industry looks forward to the Coalition Government re-firing the engines of economic reform in Australia. Over the past six years, we must acknowledge the deterioration in our international competitiveness if we are to set about sustainably remedying the problem. Abolishing the carbon tax will be a positive first step in an industry where our international competitors face no such comparable imposts.[7]

Echoing the Prime Minister, Hooke added: 'The minerals industry expects the Parliament will respect the authority the electorate has given them to abolish all elements of the carbon tax'. Hooke also repeatedly deployed the LL storyline to delegitimate the Clean Energy legislation, for example,

'The carbon tax has been a dead-weight on the economy that has failed to achieve its environmental objective while adding massive new costs on the minerals sector'.[8]

On 27 September 2013, the IPCC published its Summary for Policy-makers report. The report warned, as these reports had warned many times before, that Australia was highly vulnerability to climate impacts including catastrophic bushfires and sea level rises. Abbott's response was to deploy the LL storyline to delegitimise the Clean Energy legislation: 'under the carbon tax, measures of the former Government, our economy was damaged, but our emissions wouldn't actually reduce', adding, 'we will take effective action'.[9] Thus, Abbott's domestic intentions on climate policy were immediately clear: abolish Gillard's carbon price. Internation-ally, parallel intentions were about to be enacted.

On 2 October 2013, Prime Minister of New Zealand, John Key, visited Australia. In the aftermath of bilateral talks, neither leader publicly men-tioned climate change, carbon pricing, or anything related (which stands in stark contrast to Gillard who argued that carbon pricing in New Zealand was a model to follow).[10] The following week, on 7 October, Abbott trav-elled to Bali, Indonesia to attend the 2013 Asia Pacific Economic Cooperation (APEC) Leaders Meeting. Here, he had bilateral discussions with the leaders of Singapore, Thailand, Canada, Malaysia, Mexico, Papua New Guinea, and the US Secretary of State, John Kerry.[11] Following this, he flew to Brunei to attend the East Asia Summit (EAS).[12] At the APEC and the EAS, the Prime Minister's central message was 'Australia is open for business',[13] at no time did he publicly mention climate change, carbon pricing, energy, or anything related (once again, which was significantly apart from Gillard who routinely advocated for carbon pricing in inter-national forums).

Upon returning to Australia, the Prime Minister was asked whether his plans to abolish the carbon price came up at all during his discussions abroad. 'Yes, they did come up', Abbott confirmed, 'and I think most people are pleased to see that Australia is determined to be a low-cost business environment. The carbon tax helps to make us a high-cost environment, helps deter investment, helps to damage job growth'.[14] Simply, Abbott believed that his foreign counterparts, in general, sup-ported his view that pricing carbon was an unnecessary 'cost' (again, quite apart from Gillard who argued that the world is acting).

On 15 October 2013, the government released its Repeal of the Carbon Tax Exposure Draft Legislation.[15] Abbott deployed the CTA to help justify the draft repeal legislation: 'Abolishing the carbon tax will improve Australia's international competitiveness, which was being undermined by the unfair hit on businesses'.[16] The Draft Legislation also proposed that 'industry assistance, including the Jobs and Competitiveness Program, will continue until 30 June 2014 to assist affected businesses'.[17] So, while the price liability on big polluters would be removed, the compensation available to those same polluters would remain. This can be considered the second Critical Discourse Movement in the Abbott years because the draft repeal legislation sought to institutionalise the CTA storyline in climate policy. Abbott urged business to help refine the legislation before it was introduced into the Parliament.

In response to the Exposure Draft, the coal and gas/LNG lobbies issued formulaic public responses. They talked about the past. The MCA explained that in the past: 'The Australian minerals industry has paid almost $117 billion in company tax and royalties since 2006–07, new figures from Deloitte Access Economics (DAE) show'.[18] While the APPEA explained that 'Modelling by DAE shows that last year the industry was responsible for more than 100,000 jobs across Australia, put about $30 billion into the national economy and paid almost $8 billion in tax' – taking the added step explaining that 'that equates to the funding needs of more than 25,000 public hospital beds, or enough to cover the annual education costs of 1 million students in government primary schools'.[19]

They talked about the future. In the future, the MCA continued: 'forecasts show the value of Australia's metallurgical coal exports will grow by an average annual rate of 3.2 per cent to reach $35 billion in 2017–18'. Similarly, the APPEA continued:

> Natural gas is a 'super growth industry' that could lift Australia's next wave of economic prosperity over the next 20 years … in 2020, the industry could be contributing more than $90 billion in value added to the national economy and paying $18 billion in taxes and royalties.[20]

They also talked about the barriers to achieving this future. For the MCA there was, 'the need to tackle the structural competitiveness problem, which will determine if Australia secures maximum returns from future minerals resource development', in particular 'Abolishing the carbon tax – which adds more than $1.2 billion in deadweight costs to the mining sector – will lift some of the burden off Australia's coal sector'.[21] Similarly, the APPEA explained: 'But this (government revenue/hospital beds) will only happen if more large oil and gas projects are approved and built', and therefore

> The new Parliament must address Australia's sliding competitiveness before the potential for more big natural gas projects are lost to North America or East Africa. Australia has enormous potential supplies of

natural gas but a failure to maintain our competitive advantage through the development of natural gas will see a loss of jobs, cleaner energy and future tax revenues.[22]

Ultimately, the central message from the MCA and the APPEA was that future government revenue via royalties, as well as jobs and other economic advantages, was dependent upon competitive disadvantages being erased – particularly those imposed by the carbon price.

In late October and early November, Abbott relentlessly deployed the WW storyline to justify Labor's passing the repeal bill through the Parliament. In terms of the economic advantages, the Prime Minister asserted,

> abolishing the carbon tax would mean a 9 per cent cut in power prices, a 7 per cent cut in gas prices, a $200 a year reduction in your power bill, a $70 a year reduction in your gas bill, a $550 a year benefit to households.[23]

And in terms of the environmental advantages, Abbott continued, 'The carbon tax was never an environmental measure. Australia's domestic emissions are going up, not down, from 578 million tonnes to 621 million tonnes. That's why the carbon tax must go'.[24]

On 14 October, Bill Shorten was appointed as leader of the Labor Party and opposition leader.[25] Abbott repeatedly argued that 'Electricity Bill Shorten can either remain beholden to the Greens' and oppose the bills (which would deliver a LL scenario, Abbott maintained), or he can be 'a democrat and accept the will of the Australian people' and vote with the government to abolish this 'toxic tax' (which would deliver a WW scenario, Abbott argued).[26]

On 11 (to 23) November 2013, the Nineteenth Conference of the Parties (COP19) to the UNFCCC commenced in Warsaw, Poland. For the first time since 1997, the Australian government did not send a minister to the COP. Australia was strongly criticised by other Parties at the COP for its change of domestic position on climate change.[27] In addition, perversely, given the COP's main aim was to encourage countries to establish policies to reduce emissions, the Prime Minister used the COP as a platform to push forward his plans to abolish Australia's domestic carbon price. For example, on 12 November, the day after the COP had commenced, the Prime Minister deployed the LL storyline, from Australia – and directed towards a domestic audience – to delegitimise Australia's domestic carbon price:

> the whole problem with this carbon tax – whether it's a fixed tax or a floating tax – is that it's socialism masquerading as environmentalism.

It damages our economies, it hurts our families, it jeopardises job security and on the basis of the former Government's modelling it wasn't even going to reduce our emissions by 5 per cent. That's why we're against it.[28]

The following day, 13 November 2013, the government introduced the Clean Energy Legislation (Carbon Tax Repeal) Bill 2013 into the House of Representatives – as promised, the first bill to be introduced by an incoming Coalition Government. Abbott justified the bill to the Parliament by deploying the CTA storyline, operationalised at a local/individual level and at a national level, for example: 'repealing the Carbon Tax will reduce the cost of living, make jobs more secure and improve the competitive position of our country'.[29] Throughout the day, Abbott deployed the CTA storyline to legitimise and pressure Labor into supporting the repeal bill's passage through the Parliament, for example,

If you're fair dinkum about supporting workers job security, about saving families $550 a year, getting power bills down by $200, gas bills down by $70 a year, you will allow the carbon tax repeal legislation to go through. It's said that Bill Shorten himself would prefer to let it through.[30]

The coal and gas/LNG lobbies immediately issued media releases, both, similarly to the Prime Minister, deployed the CTA storyline (and LL storyline) to justify the immediate safe passage of the repeal bill through the Parliament.

The MCA stated:

We are calling on the parliament to avoid costly delay in the repeal of the carbon tax. The industry groups believe that Australia's high carbon tax raises business costs unnecessarily, hitting industry competitiveness and investment confidence. Delaying its removal until the new Senate sits – as would be the effect of the Opposition's current stance – would achieve nothing for the environment, but delay would add substantially to the costs and burdens facing business and households, particularly in electricity contracts. That would be deeply unhelpful as we try to build a more competitive Australia with a better chance of keeping our manufacturing base onshore.[31]

The APPEA agreed:

Industry should be allowed to start the New Year with uncertainty about the carbon tax resolved, so business can refocus on jobs and competitiveness from day one … Australia has enormous potential supplies of natural gas but if we fail to harness the opportunity to remain competitive in global markets further resources will remain undeveloped and jobs will be lost along with the potential for cheaper, cleaner energy and future tax revenues.[32]

Later in the day, former Prime Minister of Australia, Kevin Rudd, announced that he would resign from the Parliament. The 13 November 2013 is also significant because it was the next crucial step, and a step up from the draft exposure bill, in the process of institutionalising the CTA storyline as the dominant frame to understand pricing carbon in Australia – and therefore can be considered the third Critical Discourse Moment during the Abbott years.

The following week, on 21 November, the House of Representatives passed the government's bill to abolish Australia's carbon pricing legislation. Labor and the Greens opposed the bill. In response, Abbott narrowed his deployment of the CTA storyline to specifically pressure the Labor Senators to pass the repeal bill.[33] 'The House of Representatives has voted to scrap the carbon tax, and now it's up to the Senate to do the same, and I want this done by Christmas', Abbott remonstrated. Again, he repeatedly argued that Labor could side with the Coalition and the Australian people, or the Greens.[34] On 23 November, the COP19 concluded in Warsaw.

Australia's abandonment of climate diplomacy continued into December. For example, on 1 December 2013, Australia assumed the chairpersonship, and leadership role, of the G20. Abbott's hope, as he explained, was that he could tell the G20 countries in Brisbane, the city of the 2014 G20 Leaders Meeting, that 'we are getting taxes down … starting with abolishing the carbon tax'.[35] This was soon followed with a Prime Ministerial announcement on 5 December that Australia had concluded negotiations for a Free Trade Agreement (FTA) with the Republic of Korea – a top consumer of Australian coal and LNG.[36] The MCA immediately 'welcomed the landmark Free Trade Agreement with South Korea' on this basis.[37] The MCA also announced that Brendan Pearson (who is, as of November 2019, Senior Trade Policy Advisor to Prime Minister of Australia, Scott Morrison) would succeed Mitch Hooke, who would retire from as MCA Chief in December 2013.[38]

With Christmas holidays fast approaching, on 20 December 2013, the government released its Green Paper on Australia's new policy response to climate change, the centrepiece of which was the Emissions Reduction Fund (ERF). The Green Paper opened by deploying the WW storyline to legitimate the policy: The ERF, and accompanying measures such as tree planting, 'will allow Australia to enjoy the benefits of economic growth without an accompanying rise in greenhouse gas emissions'.[39] The ERF would have three simple design elements, as the Paper wrote: first, crediting emissions reductions; second, purchasing emissions reductions; and third, safeguarding emissions reductions. Put simply, the government (and taxpayers) would pay polluting industries – mostly multinational corporations – for any emissions reductions that they care to make because the scheme would be voluntary opt-in, and the safeguard mechanism would 'allow businesses to continue ordinary operations without penalty', as the Paper stated.[40] The Green Paper expressed an initial commitment of $1.55 billion to the ERF. According to Abbott and Greg Hunt, Australia's climate minister, this was a WW scheme (in contrast, Gillard and Combet deployed the WW storyline to justify a $23 a tonne price on carbon).

The CNTA storyline was not present in the Green Paper – in a first since the Howard Coalition Government. But, to accompany the WW storyline to legitimise the ERF, Hunt repeatedly deployed the CTA storyline to delegitimise Gillard's carbon price. For example, Hunt's Foreword asserted: 'The previous Government's carbon tax, whether in its fixed or floating form, essentially relies on driving up the cost of electricity and gas as its primary mechanism'.[41]

This moment in Australian climate policy marked a significant step towards the institutionalisation of the CTA storyline as the dominant frame to understand carbon pricing in Australia and can thus be understood as the fourth Critical Discourse Moment in the Abbott years.

2014

In January and February 2014, the Prime Minister attended several international events. These events made perfect platforms for the Prime Minister to pressure Labor Senators into abolishing the carbon price. On 21 January 2014, the Prime Minister arrived in Davos, Switzerland for the World Economic Forum. Here, he repeatedly argued that repealing the carbon tax was in the national interest, which was a rarity for Abbott, for example, 'Bill Shorten and the Labor Party have a chance to demonstrate whether they are serious about constructive cooperation in the national interest, and whether they are serious about abandoning their coalition with the Greens.'[42] He also deployed the CTA storyline to justify its abolition via the Senate, for example, 'the principal impact on the price of power over the last couple of years has been the carbon tax'.[43] These sentiments were reiterated at the G20 Finance Ministers meeting held in Sydney, for instance, 'scrapping bad taxes like the carbon tax' will strengthen Australia's economy;[44] and at an Australia–Canada economic forum held in Melbourne, for instance, 'Stephen Harper and I have both won elections campaigning against a carbon tax that would have killed jobs without helping the environment'.[45]

In February, the coal and gas/LNG lobbies provided submissions to ERF Green Paper. Their central concern was that the ERF ensured that competitiveness was not compromised by the policy. For example, as the MCA stated: 'of critical importance is ensuring that the new scheme does not adversely impact on the international competitiveness of Australia's export and import competing industry sectors'.[46] To achieve this, quite confidently, the MCA 'recommended a new principle – International Competitiveness – be added to the guiding principles for decision-making'.[47] Similarly the APPEA stated: 'The major challenge to the industry's continued growth is maintaining Australia's international competitiveness in the face of growing global competition'. And therefore, the APPEA, also quite confidently, explained that 'The ERF should aim to enhance Australia's international competitiveness as a destination for oil and gas investments'.[48]

Two reports in February and March pushed back against Australia's fading climate policy ambition. On 27 February, the Climate Change Authority (CCA) recommended Australia increase its emissions reduction target from 5 per cent below 2005 levels by 2020 to 19 per cent below 2000 levels by 2020 (and between 40–60 per cent below 2000 levels by 2030).[49] And on 31 March, the IPCC released its report on impacts, adaptation, and vulnerability, which highlighted Australia high vulnerability to climate impacts. In response to these events, the government deployed the LL storyline to delegitimise the carbon price and WW storyline to legitimise the ERF. For example, Greg Hunt asserted that 'The CCA shows the ineffectiveness of Labor's carbon tax. In its first year of operation, the carbon tax was a $7.6 billion hit on the Australian economy, yet emissions reduced barely 0.1 per cent'. In contrast, Hunt continued, 'the CCA report also confirms that many other countries are taking direct action to reduce emissions in ways that do not involve raising electricity prices, reducing competitiveness and hurting every single household in the country'.[50] In response to the IPCC report, Abbott stated that 'the carbon tax is a very expensive policy which has not actually reduced Australia's emissions. We want to replace it with Direct Action that really will reduce emissions without costing Western Australian families $550 a year.'[51]

By March, the Senate vote on the repeal bill loomed large. The Prime Minister obsessively deployed the CTA storyline to justify the Senate passing the bill. Almost anything in the economy was fair game for Abbott. For example, Qantas airlines announced declining profits: 'the carbon tax was a $106 million hit on Qantas. The best thing you can do for the airline industry is get rid of the carbon tax'.[52] South Australia was having an election: 'Do you really want, as Premier of South Australia (Labor), someone who thinks that the carbon tax is a fact of life?'[53] Western Australia was having a by-election: 'The question for Labor Party representatives is why are you voting in the Senate to keep the carbon tax even though it is an anti-Western Australian tax?'[54] Employment figures were released: 'I say to the Labor Party, if you're serious about trying to boost employment in this country – stop supporting this carbon tax'.[55] And on 16 March, Abbott even held a National Repeal Day in the Parliament: 'Repealing the carbon tax will improve our nation's competitiveness, help to create more jobs and lower your household costs', he maintained.[56] And finally, he threatened senators with a double dissolution election: 'the last thing the new Senate would want is to come in, refuse to give the Government its mandate and then see their career in the Senate cut short'.[57] On 19 March 2014, the Senate rejected the repeal bill. Labor and the Greens garnered 33 votes to the Coalition's 29 votes.

On 7 April 2014, Abbott visited Tokyo for a bilateral meeting with Prime Minister of Japan, Shinzo Abe. The purpose of this meeting, and the two subsequent with Korea and China, was to get assurances from Australia's three principal coal and LNG customers that their loyalty to Australia's fossil fuel industry and products would continue. It was a success. In Japan, Abbott announced a Japan–Australia Free Trade Agreement had been agreed and concluded, with 'the two leaders underlined the continued importance of stable and secure trade and investment in mineral and energy resources including liquefied natural gas and coal'.[58] The MCA's new Chief, Brendan Pearson, 'welcomed the FTA, because Japan is Australia's biggest coal customer'.[59] The next stop was Seoul, Korea. Here, on 9 April, Abbott and the President of the Republic of Korea, H.E. Park Geun-hye, formally signed the Korea–Australia FTA, which had been concluded in December 2013, and issued a 'vision statement' reaffirming both countries' commitment to the fossil fuel trade.[60] On 10 April, Abbott arrived in Shanghai. Here, Abbott hoped to 'accelerate free trade talks with China'. He argued that an FTA would be of mutual benefit:

> Australia and China have complementary strengths. Australia is already the world's number one exporter of coal. We will soon be the world's number one exporter of natural gas. This means that Australia can offer China the resource and energy security that it seeks.[61]

On 24 April, the ERF White Paper (WP) was released.[62] Minister Hunt's Foreword to the WP deployed the WW storyline to legitimise the ERF, and the CTA storyline to justify abolishing the carbon price. For example, Hunt's opened by writing: 'The Emissions Reduction Fund will achieve a cleaner environment while improving business competitiveness.' Followed by: 'the Government is repealing the carbon tax because it increased energy prices and eroded Australia's competitive advantage'.[63] As we can see however, his key message, which he expressed several times, was that Australian climate policy must, above all else, protect the competitive position of Australia's fossil fuel industry (Hunt's GP Foreword did not mention competitiveness). The WP introduction even went as far as to write: 'The ongoing development of Australia's extensive coal and gas (LNG) reserves will continue to be an important element of future growth prospects. The challenge for Australia is to reduce emissions while not damaging this valuable source of comparative advantage'.[64]

To protect the competitiveness of Australia's fossil fuel industry, the WP proposed the following:

- Crediting and purchasing of emissions, which would reward polluting industries with taxpayers' cash if they chose to voluntarily reduce their emissions. The WP allocated $2.55 billion towards this, up from the $1.55 billion allocated in the GP.
- A safeguard mechanism, which comprised four elements that protected industry competitiveness.

1 The policy would only apply to polluting facilities with direct emissions of 100,000 tonnes of CO_2-e a year or more, this meant that only 52 per cent of Australia's emissions would be covered, and about around 130 businesses (significantly less coverage than the Gillard scheme at 370 businesses).

2 Safeguard (emissions) baselines would be set using the highest level of reported emissions for a facility over the historical period. Generally, liable polluters had already altered production processes to pollute less because of the requirements of the price on carbon. But now they had licence to increase pollution back to pre-Gillard levels if they wished. In addition, the baseline would be 'flexible to accommodate any expansions in production', offering another free pass to pollute more if it could be justified on economic grounds.

3 There was a 'flexible framework for complying with the safeguard in the unlikely event of baselines being exceeded'. The WP outlined three 'flexible compliance options' (in other words 'arguments') that liable industries could use to justify why they exceeded their baseline. First, they could argue for 'an emissions-intensity test', which could be applied 'where a business emissions rise above absolute baselines, but that business can

demonstrate that its emissions-intensity of production is not rising'. Second, it could argue for 'a multi-year compliance period', which would allow for the 'averaging emissions over multiple years to be taken into account' to counter the baseline being exceeded in one particular year. Third, it could 'offset increases in their emissions by purchasing credits created by other accredited emissions reduction projects'.

4   New investments, including significant expansions to existing facilities, would simply need to 'achieve and maintain best practice'. The trouble was, as the WP wrote, 'best practice can be defined by reference to existing industry peers, or by reference to technologies employed'. In short, polluters were encouraged to define what 'best practice' meant.

•   Finally, the start date gave another free kick to big polluters. The WP explained that 'the Government will start the safeguard mechanism on 1 July 2015.... In the meantime, businesses will have the opportunity to access the Emissions Reduction Fund's crediting and purchasing elements'. So, in effect, polluting industries could access taxpayers' cash immediately, while the compliance and best practice issues were still up for negotiation.

In short, not only did the ERF design protect the competitiveness of Australia's fossil fuel industry, it actually encouraged investment in Australia's fossil fuel resources by foreign companies. In other words, the ERF rendered Australia a more attractive place for multinational fossil fuel companies to invest, compared to other resource rich countries. Cash was available to polluters, which was combined with enormous flexibility on emissions; and of course, the pending abolition of Australia's price on carbon. Shortly following the WP release, the Abbott Government's first Budget defunded the Climate Change Authority, cut $1.3 billion from the Australian Renewable Energy Agency, and allocated $1.5 billion (of the $2.55 billion) to the ERF.[65] As we shall see, Abbott's climate diplomacy would reflect this new domestic reality.

Shortly after the WP's release, (in May) the Prime Minister delivered his 2014 Annual Address to the Minerals Week Parliamentary Dinner held in Canberra. The MCA's chairman, Andrew Michelmore, introduced the Prime Minister: 'The theme of this Minerals Week is Regaining our Competitiveness', he began.[66] Followed by:

As the Prime Minister has said repeatedly, the carbon tax is a case-study in how to damage your economy for little or no environmental gain. It has reduced the international competitiveness of Australian export and import-competing industries by imposing cost burdens that none of their international competitors face. And despite the high cost paid in jobs and lost competitiveness, the environment hasn't benefitted. Like other export-focused sectors, the mining industry is looking forward to the Senate acknowledging the 2013 election outcome and voting to abolish the carbon tax.[67]

Speaking after, the Prime Minister affirmed that,

> We are determined – utterly determined – to abolish the carbon tax because, as your Chairman has just pointed out, this tax has achieved the quinella of damaging our economy without helping our environment … and if there is one fundamental problem, above all else, with the carbon tax is that it says to our people, it says to the wider world, that our coal should be left in the ground and not sold. Well really and truly, I can think of few things more damaging to our future.[68]

In June, the Prime Minister toured Europe and North America seeking foreign investment in Australia's fossil fuel industry. He had a good story to tell. He had customers lined up in Asia (FTA's with Japan, Korea, and hopefully China), and he had a domestic incentive scheme in place – the ERF – and the carbon price would soon be history. On 3 June 2014, he arrived in Paris to deliver this message. Speaking from the Australian Embassy, Abbott explained that 'the new Government in Australia is abolishing the carbon tax' along with the 'mining tax' as well as reducing company tax and environmental regulations. 'So, I want to ensure all of you that if you are looking to invest in Australia you will find a sympathetic government, which wants to constantly improve the environment in which you operate'.[69] The next stop was Canada. Before touching down in Ottawa, Abbott issued in a media release stating:

> Australia is once again open for business. The Government's drive to abolish taxes that reduce our international competitiveness, such as the carbon tax and mining tax, is making Australia an even more attractive environment for investment from Canada and the United States.[70]

While visiting Ottawa itself Abbott repeatedly deployed the LL storyline to delegitimise carbon pricing, for example: 'I've always been against a carbon tax or an emissions trading scheme because it harms our economy without necessarily helping the environment'.[71] By contrast, he sought to build a support base for his ERF (Direct Action) approach, for example, 'Direct Action is increasingly being taken right around the world, including here in North America' (again, significantly apart from Gillard who argued when visiting foreign countries that carbon pricing was on the uptick globally).[72] The Prime Minister arrived in New York in the morning of 10 June. Speaking at a business luncheon later that day he explained that:

> Australia is under new management and once more open for business. The best way to boost private sector-led growth is to get taxes down, and that's why we're abolishing the carbon tax. We have approved more than 100 major foreign investment proposals – only one has been rejected. We've also negotiated free trade agreements with Japan and Korea and hope to finalise one soon with China.[73]

In what was becoming formulaic, Abbott also repeatedly deployed the LL, WW storyline at the luncheon; and in a more aggressive turn-of-phrase from the New York Stock Exchange that afternoon: 'We're going to take direct action to get our emissions down. What we are not going to do is clobber our economy and cost jobs with things like a job-killing carbon tax'.[74] While visiting the US (and in Canada), Abbott also repeatedly sought to align his Direct Action/ERF scheme with the approach that the Obama Administration was taking, for example: 'I am encouraged that President Obama is taking what I would regard as direct action measures to reduce emissions. This is very similar to the actions that my Government proposes to take in Australia'.[75] Not incidentally because it was unable to pass a carbon pricing mechanism through the Congress.

In Washington on 12 June 2014, Abbott and President Obama delivered a joint press conference. There was no mention of climate change or energy.[76] In follow-up media engagements, Abbott was repeatedly asked whether there was any tension over climate change. 'Not at all. I regard myself as a conservationist', Abbott replied.[77]

The following day, on 13 June, Abbott arrived in Houston, Texas – the oil and gas capital of the world. The purpose of this stopover, as Abbott explained, was as follows:

> my fundamental message to the resources sector in Houston will be: Australia is open for business, we're under new management and if you want to see profitable investment opportunities look to Australia.[78]

Later that day, Abbott announced that 'Australia will open a Consulate-General in Houston in recognition of the significant two-way investment between Australia and the global energy capital'.[79] That evening, he delivered a keynote address to the Asia Society Texas Centre. Here, the Prime Minister argued that Houston and Australia had a 'common interest' in 'powering Asia's future with abundant and reliable energy' in this, 'the Asia-Pacific Century'. For Australia's part, Abbott explained, we want to become an 'affordable energy superpower'. We have abundant gas and coal, but we need foreign investment to export these resources to Asian countries, Abbott continued. The Australian government was doing its bit, domestically, by 'getting rid of unnecessary regulation', 'streamlining decision making' and 'abolishing the carbon tax', and internationally, by 'actively seeking new markets and vigorously pursuing freer trade with our key trading partners' including with Japan, South Korea, and China. In conclusion, declared the Prime Minister: 'Australia is a gateway to a region of immense opportunity' and 'Australia is open for business'.[80]

On 18 June 2014, the government introduced the Carbon Farming Initiative Amendment Bill 2014 ('the Direct Action/ERF bill') into the House of Representatives. Greg Hunt delivered a speech to the Parliament in which he repeatedly deployed the CTA and LL storylines to justify abolishing Gillard's carbon price and the WW storyline to legitimise the ERF bill.[81] For example, on the one hand, Hunt explained:

> The carbon tax was a $7.6 billion hit on the economy in its first year, yet emissions were but 0.1 per cent lower. In short, it fails to do the job. The carbon tax has led to higher electricity prices, higher gas prices and it has increased the cost of living.... It is an unnecessary burden on Australian businesses, a drag on our international competitiveness and an unfair and ineffective hit on Australian families. For these reasons the government has moved to abolish the carbon tax as a fundamental priority since coming to office.

Yet, on the other hand, he continued:

> Unlike the approach under the carbon tax, the Emissions Reduction Fund will provide positive incentives to help Australian businesses and households lower their energy costs, improve their agricultural productivity and increase their efficiency.[82]

Hunt's speech, which commenced the passage of the ERF as Australia's cornerstone domestic climate policy, can be understood as the fifth and final Critical Discourse Moment in the Abbott years. Its eventual passage through the Senate enshrined the CTA storyline into law as the dominant frame to understand carbon pricing in Australia: pricing carbon was an unnecessary 'cost' – soon, it would be the law of the land.

The following week, on 23 June 2014, the government re-introduced the Clean Energy Legislation (Carbon Tax Repeal) bill into the House of Representatives. The Prime Minister's speech to the House was, in part, replete with the LL storyline to justify the passage of the bill, for example: 'scrapping the carbon tax is a vital part of this Government's Economic Action Strategy because the carbon tax is bad for jobs, it hurts families and it doesn't help the environment'.[83] And in part, replete with the WW storyline to legitimise the Direct Action/ERF replacement, for example:

> We'll scrap the carbon tax and then proceed with our Direct Action Plan. The centrepiece of this Direct Action Plan will be the Emissions Reduction Fund. It's an incentive-based approach that will support Australian businesses and households at the same time as reducing Australia's emissions.[84]

In this speech, as we can see, Abbott explicitly acknowledged that repealing the carbon price was central to the government's economic agenda, which overall, was designed to enhance the competitive position of Australia compared to foreign countries, by lowering taxation (removing the so-called carbon and mining taxes, and lowering company tax) and removing regulations (e.g. establishing a 'one-stop shop' for environmental approvals) – and in doing so, attract foreign investors to Australia's shores. 'Repealing the carbon tax improves the competitive position of our country', Abbott's speech to the Parliament concluded, 'Now why would anyone be against that'.[85]

Two days later, on 25 June 2014, Clive Palmer – Australian mining billionaire, vocal climate science sceptic, Member of Parliament, and leader of the Palmer United Party (PUP), which would hold two seats and the balance of power in the new Senate commencing on 1 July 2014 – and eminent climate campaigner and the former US Vice President, Al Gore, held a joint press conference in Canberra broadcast live to a national audience. Here, Palmer announced that his PUP Senators would pass the government's carbon price repeal bill but would not support cuts to the Clean Energy Finance Corporation or abolish the Climate Change Authority.[86] On 27 June, the repeal bill passed the House of Representatives.

On 1 July 2014, the repeal bill was re-introduced into the Australian Senate. 'I expect all of the crossbench senators to be true to their pre-election commitments' and pass the bill, asserted the Prime Minister.[87] This remark was principally directed towards the PUP Senators, and Clive Palmer himself, all of whom were vocal about the importance of repealing the legislation before the Federal Election. But the Prime Minister was circumspect nonetheless: 'Mr Palmer, spectacularly, declared last week that he was going to vote to repeal the carbon tax. But I never count my chickens until they've hatched'.[88]

Over the following weeks, while the repeal bill was debated in the Senate again, the Prime Minister mercilessly deployed the CTA and LL storyline to keep the pressure on PUP Senators. For example, in the first instance, 'It's a bad tax, it's a toxic tax, it's making our businesses less competitive, it's making household costs higher and the sooner we're rid of it the better',[89] and in the second instance, 'the Coalition has fought hard to scrap this toxic tax – we know it hurts jobs, it hurts families and it does nothing at all for the environment'.[90] Similarly to Abbott's efforts to pressure Labor in the previous Senate, he presented new senators with a choice: On the one hand, senators could side with 'the Australian people' and the government who wanted to 'scrap this toxic tax' (and deliver a WW scenario). Or, on the other hand, they could side with Labor and the Greens 'who love this tax' (and deliver a LL scenario).[91]

On 17 July 2014, the Australian Senate passed the Coalition's bill to repeal Australia's price on carbon pollution (but blocked the accompanying CEFC or CCA abolition bills). This was the first time, globally, that a developed country had abolished a legislated price on carbon pollution. 'If I could address the Australian people', Abbott told the press pack, as he turned to speak directly down the camera:

> In September last year, you voted to scrap the tax, and today, the Parliament finally listened. Today, the world's biggest carbon tax that you voted to get rid of is finally gone. A useless, destructive tax which damaged jobs, which hurt families cost of living and which didn't actually help the environment is finally gone.[92]

The coal and gas/LNG lobbies responded in kind. The MCA's Chief, Brendan Pearson, asserted: 'The removal of the world's biggest carbon tax is an important step towards regaining the competitive edge that Australia lost over the last decade.'[93] Similarly, the APPEA's Chief, David Byers, asserted: 'Today's repeal of the carbon pricing mechanism is significant as it removes a cost facing Australian LNG exporters competing in global markets; one that does not exist for our international competitors.'[94] Simply, the MCA, the APPEA and the federal government agreed that, above all else, repealing carbon price would enhance the competitive position of Australian industry compared to foreign countries, and in doing so, help encourage foreign investment, boost jobs, and increase government revenue.

But while building a competitive Australia to encourage coal and gas investment was a part of Abbott's climate and energy plan, to become the 'affordable energy capital of the world', he would also facilitate the expansion of Australia's uranium export industry. On 4 September, the Prime Minister arrived in Mumbai for bilateral talks with the Prime Minister of India, Narendra Modi. 'I want Australia to be an energy superpower', Abbott told the Mumbai press, 'We have large reserves of uranium. We have massive reserves of coal. We have extensive reserves of gas', he continued. After talks the with Modi the following day, 5 September, a joint statement was released that 'welcomed the signing of the bilateral Civil Nuclear Cooperation Agreement' for the export of Australian uranium to India, and also affirmed that Australia's coal and gas reserves, as well as uranium, would help provide for India's energy security for decades to come.[95] Abbott described the controversial Adani mine as 'one of the minor miracles of our time' based on its capacity to 'power the lives of 100 million Indians' – I hope it goes ahead, Abbott confirmed.[96]

The other critical component of Abbott's diplomatic strategy on climate and energy, which was ultimately designed to advance the interests of Australia's mining industry, was to snub the UN climate negotiations. Towards the end of the month, on 23 September 2014, world leaders, including the US President Barack Obama and UK Prime Minister David Cameron, Australia's traditional allies, attended the UN's annual Climate Summit held at its headquarters in New York.[97] Abbott did not attend, 'Foreign Minister, Julie Bishop, will ably represent Australia', he remarked.[98] Instead, he arrived in New York the following day, on 24 September, to deliver his Address, alongside other world leaders, to the UNGA. In a press conference prior to the Address he told reporters what they can expect: 'I guess what I want to do is remind the world of what a good global citizen Australia has been'.[99] In the Address itself, the Prime Minister explained that 'As this year's chair of the G20, our agenda is to strengthen the world economy. Rather than preaching, we're trying to lead by example. Australia has abolished the carbon tax.'[100] The G20 would be held in Brisbane in November 2014.

In October 2014, Abbott toured the country deploying the CTA storyline to justify the abolition of Australia's carbon price, something that he had achieved four months prior. In Canberra, he said, 'Well, the carbon tax is gone, this will reduce your costs and improve business competitiveness'.[101] In Sydney, 'The job of government is to try to make it easier for businesses to compete and to flourish. That's why we scrapped the carbon tax'.[102] In Queensland, 'The carbon tax would have killed the coal industry. I'm here to affirm my faith and confidence in the coal industry'.[103] Also in Sydney, 'The carbon tax is gone. [And] we've stopped the demonisation of coal because coal is the world's lowest cost power source.'[104] Direct Action was hardly mentioned by the Prime Minister. Despite this, on 31 October 2014, the Coalition's Direct Action Plan, with its ERF as its centrepiece, passed the Senate.[105] Later in the day, the APPEA released a media release titled: 'ERF detail crucial for international competitiveness'.[106] Their principal concern was that the safeguard mechanism, which was yet to be finalised, would not fully protect their LNG exporters: 'It needs to ensure Australian production of cleaner energy, such as natural gas, is not burdened with additional costs not faced by foreign competitors', the APPEA explained. The MCA did not respond directly to the Senate vote. Instead, on 31 October, they released a booklet titled, Minerals Industry Priorities and Regularity Reforms, which detailed a systemic economy-wide package of 'reforms' to improve the competitiveness of the minerals and mining industry, including in the areas of 'environmental approvals', 'workplace relations', 'coastal shipping', 'business taxation', among several others, including of course 'climate and energy', which delivered a range of messages similarly to the following:

> Notwithstanding subsequent rationalisation of measures, and the removal of the carbon tax, energy and climate change schemes continue to add direct costs to companies. The regulatory cost of such measures arises most directly in the form of higher electricity costs, eroding Australia's traditional competitive advantage in relatively affordable and reliable energy supply.[107]

For the MCA, Abbott's Prime Ministership presented an immense opportunity to implement economy-wide competitive-based reforms that favoured the mining industry. They pushed this agenda hard from June to October of 2014, releasing wide-ranging reports, such as Australia's Competitiveness: Reversing the Slide,[108] and building coalitions with other industry groups to achieve specific objectives, for example, to pressure the Parliament to implement a 'one-stop-shop' for environmental approvals, which they argued were 'one of the biggest drags on Australia's international competitiveness'.[109] But Abbott's political fortunes were about to take a significant turn for the worse.

On 10 November 2014, the Prime Minister arrived in Beijing for the APEC Leaders' Meeting. Shortly after, Abbott and US President Obama held a joint press conference. Climate change was not mentioned.[110] Two days later, on 12 November, President Obama and the President of China, Xi Jinping, issued The US–China Joint Announcement on Climate Change, which would commit both countries to reducing their net GHG emissions by 26–28 per cent below 2005 levels by the year 2025.[111]

The Announcement signalled that the 'North–South' (US–China) standoff that had wreaked havoc at the Copenhagen climate talks in 2009 would be potentially overcome at the Twenty-First Conference of the Parties (COP21) to be held in Paris in 2015.

Abbott and Australia looked out-of-step, isolated, and excluded on climate change (similarly to John Howard and Australia in 2007). Which was confirmed the following day by the Prime Minister himself: 'Look, we've just had the APEC conference in Beijing and climate change was hardly mentioned – hardly mentioned', he told journalists.[112] Once cognisant of the US–China announcement Abbott was furious, and journalists were on the attack. Will Australia now increase its greenhouse gas reduction target, Mr Abbott? – 'our target remains a 5% cut in emissions', Abbott remonstrated.[113] Will you now include climate change on the G20 Agenda? – 'The UN deals with climate change. The G20 is an economic conference', he replied.[114]

Australia's coal and gas/LNG lobbies were honing their arguments for the G20. For the MCA, Australian coal exports were critical to 'lifting hundreds of millions of people out of energy poverty' in India and Southeast Asia.[115] For the APPEA, Australian LNG exports were critical to providing 'flexible and reliable lower-emissions energy to drive economic growth as well as reductions in emissions' in Japan, China, and South Korea.[116] In short, Australia's coal and LNG exporters had divided the Asia-Pacific region into providing cheap coal for poor counties, and more expensive, yet cleaner, LNG for richer countries. A point that brought minor discord. For example, the MCA remarked, 'the cost of generating electricity from coal is half the cost of gas', while the APPEA countered, 'natural gas is a much cleaner-burning fuel than traditional energy sources'.[117] Both lobbies released a string of commissioned reports and citied experts to help validate their arguments.[118]

On 15 November 2014, the G20 got underway in Brisbane. Abbott's opening remarks at the First Plenary did not mention climate change, rather, the G20's purpose was to 'deliver more jobs, more growth and freer trade'.[119] That afternoon, the US President, Barack Obama, delivered a speech to a packed stadium at the University of Queensland, in which he deployed the environmental CNTA to justify stronger action by all nations, including Australia:

> As we focus on our economy, we cannot forget the need to lead on the global fight against climate change. Here in the Asia Pacific, nobody has more at stake when it comes to thinking about and then acting on climate change. Here, a climate that increases in temperature will mean more extreme and frequent storms, more flooding, rising seas

that submerge Pacific islands. Here in Australia, it means longer droughts, more wildfires. The incredible natural glory of the Great Barrier Reef is threatened. Worldwide, this past summer was the hottest on record. No nation is immune, and every nation has a responsibility to do its part.... The United States and Australia has a lot in common. One of the things we have in common is we produce a lot of carbon. Part of it's this legacy of wide-open spaces and the frontier mentality, and this incredible abundance of resources. And so, historically, we have not been the most energy-efficient of nations, which means we've got to step up.[120]

In its wake, Abbott outwardly supported enhanced climate action. But behind the scenes, he was advancing the interests of the fossil fuel industry. For example, on 17 November, in a morning press conference, Abbott explained: 'obviously, it goes without saying that G20 leaders – all of us – support strong and effective action to address climate change'.[121] That afternoon, with German Chancellor, Angela Merkel, Abbott remarked: 'Climate change is real, humanity does have a significant impact, and we have got to take strong and effective action'.[122] However, later in the day, after meeting with President Xi Jinping, Abbott announced the completion of negotiations for a China-Australia Free Trade Agreement, which, he explained means 'tariffs on coking coal will be removed on day one, with the tariff on thermal coal phasing out over two years'.[123]

The following day, on 18 November, Abbott held a joint press conference with Prime Minister of India, Narendra Modi: 'If all goes to plan' Abbott explained, 'next year, an Indian company will begin Australia's largest ever coal development, the Adani mine, which will light the lives of 100 million Indians for the next half century ... and Australia will export uranium to India'.[124] On 19 November, Abbott held a joint press conference with President of France, François Hollande: 'I raised climate change because it's very important that we get strong and effective outcomes from the conference in Paris next year', Abbott remarked.[125] The G20 Leaders' Summit Communique comprised several points on reducing emissions and the importance of negotiating a global deal on climate change, for example:

We will work together to adopt successfully a protocol, another legal instrument or an agreed outcome with legal force under the UNFCCC that is applicable to all parties at the 21st Conference of the Parties (COP21) in Paris in 2015.[126]

The Prime Minister, and his Trade Minister, Andrew Robb (who had a history of vocal scepticism about the veracity of consensus climate science) had now concluded FTA's with Australia's three top coal and LNG consumers – Japan, Korea, and China. The MCA's Brendan Pearson was thrilled: 'We applaud the work of Prime Minister Tony Abbott and Trade Minister Andrew Robb in completing an outstanding job to secure this outcome with three North Asian economic powerhouses – Korea, Japan and China', he explained – 'At the national level, these agreements will be an important contributor to Australian prosperity over the next three decades', he added.[127] The MCA's Deputy Chief Executive, John Kunkel (who is, as of November 2019, Chief-of-Staff to Prime Minister of Australia, Scott Morrison), attended the signing ceremony.[128] The MCA also released a Fact Sheet that showed the value of Australian coal exports to each country per year (Japan $17.7 billion per year. China $7.5 billion per year. Korea $5 billion per year).[129]

The Twentieth Conference of the Parties (COP20) was held in Lima, Peru, between 1 and 14 December 2014. The Prime Minister did not attend. Australia's Foreign Minister, Julie Bishop (the only woman in the Federal Cabinet), would lead the delegation, but she would be chaperoned by Andrew Robb. Robb's attendance at the COP20 was widely reported as to avoid Bishop committing Australia to a process or a deal that may have negative domestic economic consequences. Abbott brushed off this charge: 'For the Warsaw conference (COP19) we were criticised for not sending a minister, now at the Lima conference, it seems we're in trouble for sending two Ministers'.[130]

On 10 December, Australia announced that it would contribute $200 million over four years to the UN Green Climate Fund – its flagship announcement at the COP. The Prime Minister deployed the WW story-line to legitimise this contribution: 'All countries should take practical and proportionate steps to take action on climate change while safeguarding economic growth'.[131] The cash would be appropriated from Australia's foreign aid budget and used to advance regional reforestation programmes. The carbon credits generated by these programmes could then be used to offset any increase in Australia's emissions reduction target.[132] 'Any new post-2020 target would be announced in mid-2015', Abbott remarked later in the day.[133]

For the remainder of December 2014, Abbott came under increasing political pressure at home.

He had been exposed as out-of-step internationally on climate change. Australia's emissions were clearly rising, after declining during the Gillard years. He was widely accused of breaking election promises on taxation, similarly to Gillard. His 2014 Budget was being judged across the political spectrum as unquestionably harsh – particularly towards the unemployed and pensioners. He was facing increasingly bad polls. And journalists, once again in Australian politics, were asking about internal leadership challenges. In response, Abbott went into campaigning mode, repeatedly listing his achievements, which almost always included deploying the CTA storyline to justify removing Australia's carbon price, which had occurred six months prior.[134]

2015

For Abbott, January 2015 proved disastrous. Early polls indicated that the former leader of the Liberal Party, Malcolm Turnbull – who Abbott had replaced as opposition leader in December 2009 – was significantly more popular with voters than the Prime Minister. In response, Abbott continued to deploy the CTA storyline to legitimise the abolition of the carbon price, and by implication, justify the continuation of his Prime Ministership. For example, 'Judge us on our record. We said we'd get rid of the carbon tax – and we did. That's $550 a year extra for families'.[135] And on 26 January, Australia Day, the Prime Minister made a politically fatal mistake (it was Abbott's 'no carbon tax' moment) by awarding a Knighthood (a title that he himself had recently exhumed) to Prince Philip – The Queen of England's husband.[136] A storm of criticism ensued. Abbott was accused of 'poor judgement', 'having an unhealthy devotion to the Royal Family', and failing to consult with Cabinet on the decision, a charge that he confirmed – 'this was a Captain's Pick', he said.[137] The Prime Minister had become 'a national joke', traditional media loyalists remarked. Speculation was building that Abbott wouldn't lead the Liberal Party to the next election – 'absolute nonsense', Abbott retorted.[138]

From 1 to 4 February, speculation intensified that Abbott would be imminently replaced as leader of the Liberal Party and Prime Minister. In response, he repeatedly deployed the CTA storyline on carbon pricing to legitimise his ongoing leadership of the Party.[139] On 5 February, it was reported that Abbott would not be Prime Minister by next week. 'I'm very confident I will be', he replied, 'I know my colleagues and I trust my colleagues'.[140] The following day, Abbott announced: 'Well, two of my colleagues have called for a leadership spill' which will take place on 9 February.[141] From 6 to 8 February, Abbott campaigned to keep his job. He deserved to remain leader, he told colleagues via the media, principally because he had abolished the carbon price (by contrast, Gillard justify her incumbency on the basis that she had 'priced carbon' – see Chapter 3).[142] On 9 February 2015 at 9:00 am the Liberal Party Room met to decide the fate Tony Abbott. The motion to spill the leadership was proposed. And it was defeated 61 votes to 39. There was to be no challenge. Tony Abbott remained Prime Minister. 'This matter is now behind us', Abbott remarked afterwards.[143] Abbott's second chance was premised on him altering his political messaging from predominantly negative and oppositional to positive and Prime Ministerial. But instead of changing, Abbott doubled down.

For the remainder of February, Abbott toured the country deploying the CTA storyline to justify the abolition of the carbon price, which had occurred eight months prior. In Canberra, on 11 February, the Prime Minister asserted, 'Australia is a vastly more attractive investment destination now than 8 months ago because the carbon tax is gone'.[144] In Melbourne, 'the good news for pensioners is that they've lost the carbon tax, but they keep all the carbon tax compensation'.[145] In Sydney, 'the abolition of the carbon tax was obviously very good for some small businesses because they use a lot of power'.[146] In Brisbane, 'we abolished the carbon tax to put $550 a year back in the pockets of Australian families'.[147] Later in Brisbane, 'we've scrapped the anti-Queensland carbon tax'.[148] In Adelaide, 'this Government has abolished the carbon tax which has certainly reduced the power bills'.[149] And in Darwin on 21 February, 'the carbon tax is gone, that means that $550 a year more is in the pockets of Australian families'.[150] Direct Action was hardly mentioned. By the end of February, questions about a second leadership challenge emerged.[151] 'I know the media like to hyperventilate about Canberra insider gossip, but I'm not going to play that game', Abbott replied.

In March, Abbott continued to boast about abolishing the carbon price. The benefits included lower power prices, as well as saving families and pensioners $550 per year – the same as last month. But several new justifications emerged, mostly relating to reducing taxes and the government's achievements. In the first instance, for example, in Kalgoorlie, Western Australia, on 10 March, the Prime Minister stated that he opposed increasing the royalty rate on gold mining because 'I want to see less tax, not more tax. That's why we abolished the carbon tax'.[152] In Geelong, the Prime Minister argued that he opposed Labor's planned tax increase on superannuation because 'we want lower, simpler, fairer taxes and we have made a very good start by scrapping the carbon tax'.[153] In Tasmania, Abbott explained that he opposed 'bracket creep' (increase tax liability due to increased wages) because 'this Government wants to get taxes down. We've got rid of the carbon tax.'[154] In the second instance, for example, in Melbourne, he argued that he should remain Liberal leader because 'we delivered on our election commitments – the carbon tax is gone'.[155] In Canberra, he argued that 'this Government is fixing Labor's mess. We scrapped the carbon tax.' Later in Canberra, he added 'this is a Government which keeps its commitments. We said we'd scrap the carbon tax – we have.'[156] Direct Action was hardly mentioned.

In April, it continued.[157] New justifications mostly involved taxation. The Former Liberal Treasurer, Peter Costello, 'is perfectly entitled to his view on the Budget, but this is a tax-cutting Government as we've already demonstrated by abolishing the carbon tax'. The national accounts figures showed strong growth, 'which doesn't happen by accident. It happens because you've got a Government which is putting the right policies in place. The carbon tax is gone', Abbott explained. But also, how do you expect families to pay for sky-rocketing child care in Sydney? 'Well, I want to see families better able to deal with cost-of-living pressures and that's why we abolished the carbon tax', Abbott replied.[158] In terms of power bills, Abbott explained, 'right around our country, in shops and cafes, in manufacturing plants and transport businesses, I've been shown electricity and gas bills that were smaller because there is no carbon tax anymore'.[159] Direct Action was hardly mentioned.

In March and April, the government's process was in train to determine Australia's GHG emissions reduction target for the post-2020 period. On 28 March 2015, the government invited submissions to the process. Any new target would have to deliver a WW scenario, the Prime Minister asserted, for example: 'We are determined to reduce emissions – but without a carbon tax and without destroying jobs'.[160] In April, the MCA and the APPEA entered their submissions to the process. For both lobbies, Australia's post-2020 target, and accompanying domestic measures to meet that target, must be comparable to competitor nations, which are unlikely to implement a carbon constraint on their businesses any time soon, they argued. As the MCA's submission explained:

> In taking on new domestic and international emissions commitments, it is critical that new layers of cost added to the economy through additional abatement commitments are roughly in line with the costs borne by comparable countries.... It is fundamental to note that Australia competes mostly, though not exclusively, with developing nations, who will be under less pressure to commit to ambitious targets.[161]

Similarly, the APPEA's submission explained:

> One of the key factors to consider when assessing any changes to Australia's emissions reduction targets is the action or inaction of LNG trade competitors.... Analysis shows that none of Australia's major LNG competitors have policies in place that impose an 'effective' carbon price on their LNG exporters. Further, the prospect of our competitors taking meaningful action in the foreseeable future is low.[162]

In terms of the precise domestic measures to meet the post-2020 target, the MCA and the APPEA differed in their priorities. The MCA argued that the domestic measures must be 'incentive-based rather than punitive' for example government funding provided to industry through the ERF or put towards developing Carbon Capture and Storage (CCS) or High Efficiency Low Emission (HELE) technologies. These measures would ensure that national climate policy 'did not adversely impact the competitiveness of Australia's export and import competing sectors and broader economy', asserted the MCA.[163] In contrast, the APPEA argued that 'most crucially, the APPEA supports a national climate policy that delivers abatement at least cost', which means 'any national approach should recognise the widest possible range of credible offsets, including those sourced overseas'. Allowing this measure would help 'maintain the competitiveness of Australian export industries, particularly cleaner global contributor exports such as the LNG industry', asserted the APPEA.[164]

In terms of the impact of national climate policy that failed to protect industry competitiveness, the MCA and the APPEA once again converged. The MCA's submission asserted that it 'would damage the minerals and energy industry that account for more than half of Australia's total exports, and would have negative implications for the wider economy as well as for government revenue'.[165] The APPEA submission asserted that it 'would compromise the LNG industry that creates significant wealth for the country, including through the employment of many Australians, and underpins the revenue collections of governments and generates valuable export revenue for the Australian economy'.

In May the government delivered its second Budget. The Treasurer, Joe Hockey, confirmed in his Budget speech to the Parliament: 'In the next five years we will become the world's largest exporter of liquified natural gas'. It was a green light for gas. The APPEA took this as 'the Federal Budget highlighting the importance of a growing oil and gas industry for the economic wellbeing of all Australians'.[166] The APPEA's annual conference held shortly after was a confident affair. The APPEA's chairman Bruce Lake opened the conference: 'We have at least 40 more years of LNG shipments. But we are also developing new technologies – such as floating LNG platforms – that let us tap previously inaccessible resources'.[167] There was no end in sight for Australia's LNG exports. The APPEA lobbyist, and former Industry Minister in the Gillard Government, Martin Ferguson, closed the conference: 'Our industry has achieved great things. We can do even more providing that both industry and government play their parts on cost and competitiveness challenges.'[168] On 12 May, Malcolm Roberts replaced David Byers as the APPEA's Chief Executive.

On 3 June, the Prime Minister delivered his 2015 Annual Address to the MCA's Minerals Week Annual Parliamentary Dinner. 'This Government does have a clear vision for mining', Abbott began, and it was this:

> This Government wants our country to have the most competitive and advanced mining industry of any developed democracy. Under this Government, the carbon tax has gone. Free trade agreements have been concluded with China, Japan and Korea. So, we have made it easier to do business, but it doesn't stop there. John Howard often said that our national competitiveness was like a race with an ever-receding finishing line. Our goal is to make our resources industry the most competitive in the world.[169]

Following this, the Prime Minister reassured the audience not to worry about the upcoming Paris climate negotiations or Australia's post-2020 target because 'the Emissions Reduction Fund has so far achieved 47 million tonnes of reduction at a cost of just $14 a tonne. And we will continue to deliver reduced emissions [not "reduce emission"] in ways that don't damage our economy.'[170]

From May to July 2015, Abbott continued to campaign against the 'carbon tax', which as of May, had been abolished for eleven months. In May, in the wake of the Budget he repeated, over and over, that the carbon price was a 'tax' which was inconsistent with his 'low-taxing' government – and 'that's why it had to go'.[171] On 19 May, the Labor opposition announced that if elected it might re-establish a domestic price carbon. Abbott pounced, repeatedly deploying the CTA and LL storylines throughout the remainder of May, all of June, and to mid-July, to delegitimise Labor's suggestion. For example, on 20 May 2015:

> So, while the Budget from this Government was about cutting tax, I notice yesterday that we had the Labor Party recommitting to a carbon tax. So, you've got a very clear contrast between a Government which wants to help business and help jobs by cutting tax, and an Opposition which wants to hurt business and hurt jobs by increasing tax.[172]

On 5 June, for example, Abbott asserted: 'The difference between this Government and our political opponents is that we will reduce emission without smashing the economy with a great big new tax on everything'.[173] And for example on 11 July:

> We scrapped the carbon tax – which was a useless and unnecessary burden on business, and a useless and unnecessary burden on

everyone. We are never going to hit you with a great big jobs-destroying carbon tax, which, of course, is the first thing that any re-elected Labor government might do.[174]

By contrast, Abbott repeatedly deployed the WW storyline to legitimise the government's Direct Action/ERF approach, which was seldom mentioned until after Labor's suggested return to a carbon price, for example, on 15 July 2015, Abbott asserted: 'This Government, through Direct Action, is securing very strong reductions in emissions without damaging the economy'.[175] On 19 July, Labor held its national conference and formally re-committed to establishing a national ETS if elected to government. Abbott went ballistic:

> Labor's ETS might as well be called an electricity tax scam, because that's what it is, an electricity tax scam that will be scamming the consumers of Australia for years and years and decades and decades if it was to be put in place.[176]

Quite apart from criticising Labor, over this period Abbott also managed to think of new ways to justify the repeal of the carbon price. Should land taxes be increased? 'As far as this Government is concerned, we want taxes that are lower. That is why we scrapped the carbon tax', Abbott replied.[177] Why has your government taken until now to discuss reforming the Federation? 'Well, we've done quite a lot over the last two years. We've scrapped the carbon tax', Abbott replied. Is your government out of touch with the public? 'If you actually look at what we've done, we've got rid of the hated carbon tax', he replied.[178]

By August, the government was close to announcing the emissions reduction target that Australia would take to the COP21 negotiations. On 9 August 2015, Abbott deployed the WW storyline to pre-emptively legitimate the target, and the domestic measures that would achieve it: 'We will continue to make a strong and responsible contribution to the global effort to address climate change, but we'll do this without sacrificing jobs or prosperity', adding 'through the Direct Action policy, we're taking sensible action here at home to improve the local environment and reduce emissions'.[179]

Two days later, on 11 August 2015, the Prime Minister announced that Australia would reduce GHG emissions by 26–28 per cent below 2005 levels by 2030. In his press conference, Abbott repeatedly deployed the WW storyline to legitimise the target and the LL storyline to delegitimise Labor's approach:

We have got to reduce our emissions, but we have got to reduce our emissions in ways which are consistent with continued strong growth, particularly with continued strong jobs growth. The last thing we want to do is strengthen the environment and at the same time damage our economy – that is the Labor way, to put the environment ahead of the economy. What we want to do is to protect and promote both and that is exactly what today's decision is all about.[180]

The Prime Minister, as well as Greg Hunt and Julie Bishop, who accompanied the Prime Minister, all stressed that Australia's target was consistent with comparable economies: For example, Abbott affirmed,

Our 26 to 28 per cent target, it's better than Japan. It's almost the same as New Zealand. It's a whisker below Canada. It's a little below Europe. It's about the same as the United States. It's vastly better than Korea. And, of course, it is unimaginably better than China. So this is fairly and squarely in the middle of comparable economies.[181]

While the Prime Minister did not mention Direct Action himself, the accompanying media release clarified that 'The Government will meet Australia's 2030 target through policies built on the successful Direct Action plan, in particular the Emissions Reduction Fund and its Safeguard Mechanism'.[182] The explanatory memorandum to complete the package of deliverables on the day, added: 'acting in concert with others, and choosing low cost policy options, means we can contribute while remaining competitive and protecting our economy and jobs'.[183]

The coal and gas/LNG lobbies issued mixed responses. The MCA's Brendan Pearson described the target as 'credible and appropriate but one that will impose strains on the Australian economy, especially export and import-competing industries'. He rejected the proposition that is was comparable with other countries, rather 'the reality is that it will impose a higher cost on the Australian economy than that borne by comparable developed nations including the United States, Canada and the European Union'. But ultimately, he suggested, the cost borne by industry will be determined by the domestic policy measures, and their design, and therefore 'the minerals sector is committed to working with the Australian Government on the policy measures that will be adopted to achieve the proposed targets'.[184]

The APPEA also acknowledged the post-2020 target but, similarly to the MCA, was ultimately focused on the domestic measures, and their design: 'the Government's final 2030 emissions reduction commitment will require reducing emissions by about 900 million tonnes from 2020 to

2030. The policies and programs that might be used to deliver this commitment remain a key area of ongoing focus'.[185] The APPEA was particularly concerned about the final design of the Safeguard Mechanism, which 'must not impose costs on Australian producers that inhibit industry growth or are not faced by our competitors', asserted Malcolm Roberts. A design that failed to protect LNG exporters, he warned, risked forgoing 'jobs, royalties and exports'. 'We look forward to working constructively to improve the operation of the mechanism', Roberts concluded.[186] Simply, for both lobbies, the domestic policy measures, not the national target, would ultimately determine industry competitiveness.

For the remainder of August and early September, the Prime Minister repeatedly deployed the WW storyline to sell the government's new target, for example, on 15 August, he explained that:

> This week we declared our target for 2030. A 26–28 per cent reduction of emissions on 2005 levels – 26–28 per cent. So, let's not have anyone say that this is a Government which is indifferent to environmental outcomes. This Government cares passionately about the environment. We only have one planet. We must leave it in better shape for our children and our grandchildren but the last thing we should ever do is clobber the economy to protect the environment. Our 2030 target is economically responsible, it's environmentally responsible.[187]

And he continued to campaign against Gillard's carbon price which was ancient history in political terms, abolished more than 14 months prior. Nonetheless, in this period, Abbott miraculously managed to invent new iterations[188] of the CTA storyline to justify its removal, which can be bundled into three themes – by-election voting, the economy, and leadership of the Liberal Party. In the first instance, the Federal seats of Canning in Western Australia, and Indi in Victoria, were up for grabs. In Western Australia, Abbott twice toured the state campaigning for the Liberal candidate. His core message was:

> We've got a very strong record when it comes to helping Western Australia. We've removed an anti-Western Australian carbon tax. If Labor were to come back to government, the carbon tax comes back, only it's the carbon tax on steroids. So, if the people of Canning want to protect their state from an anti-Western Australian tax, they should be voting for the Liberal candidate.[189]

In Indi, he campaigned for the re-election of outspoken climate science sceptic Sophie Mirabella: 'She was one the leaders of the campaign against the carbon tax – a very successful campaign against the carbon tax', he explained.[190]

In terms of the economy, Abbott explained, foreign companies want to invest in Australia because of 'the substantial tax cuts that this Government has put in place, particularly the loss of the carbon tax'.[191] Employment has risen 'at least in part due to the successful Government policy to repeal the carbon tax'.[192] BHP mining may expand its operations because 'while I can't wave a magic wand and get BHP to commit, I can do things that make it easier like when we abolished the carbon tax'.[193] We oppose Labor's Bank Deposit Tax because 'this Government is in the business of protecting Australians' savings – not raiding them. We have scrapped the carbon tax.'[194] We are supporting 'hardworking Australians in our country who are having a go. That's why we repealed the carbon tax – a useless handbrake on economic activity'.[195]

In terms of the leadership of the Liberal Party. Is the Canning by-election a test of your leadership? 'On the test of could we get the carbon tax repealed, we passed', Abbott replied.[196] How do you respond to polls that put Malcolm Turnbull ahead of you as preferred Prime Minister? 'This is a Government which is focused on delivering better outcomes to the people of Australia and the great thing about the abolition of the carbon tax is that it has delivered to households', he said.[197]

On 6 September, the Prime Minister, and most of the Liberal/National Coalition Party, celebrated its two-year anniversary. The Prime Minister celebratory press conference was a litany of language that he had deployed on carbon pricing since becoming Prime Minister.[198]

The following week, on 10 September 2015, the Prime Minister visited Papua New Guinea for talks with Pacific Island leaders. Climate change was on the agenda. 'I've got a very good story to tell on climate change', Abbott remarked from Port Moresby, 'we have pledged a 26 to 28 per cent cut by 2030. So, I think Pacific leaders should be reassured by the seriousness with which Australia is approaching this issue'.[199] The following day, on 11 September 2015, in Queensland, in reference to a late arrival to the meeting, the Prime Minster quipped, 'we had a bit of that up in Port Moresby', to which Australia's Immigration Minister, Peter Dutton (who is, as of November 2019, Home Affairs Minister in the Morrison Government), responded: 'time doesn't mean anything when you're about to have water lapping at your door'. The Prime Minister laughed awkwardly as the Treasurer, Scott Morrison (who is, as of November 2019, Prime Minister of Australia), leant in: 'there's a boom microphone up there'.[200]

Three days later, on 14 September, at 4:00 pm, Malcolm Turnbull, held a press conference to announce that he would resign from the Cabinet, effective immediately, and challenge Tony Abbott to the leadership of the Liberal Party and by implication, to the Prime Ministership. He cited the government's consistent poor polling, poor economic leadership, and the absence of 'a style of leadership that respects people's intelligence' as the principal justifications for his challenge. The vote took place that evening at 9:15 pm. Turnbull won the leadership spill 54 votes to 44, becoming leader of the Liberal Party. On 15 September 2015, Malcolm Turnbull was sworn-in as the 29th Prime Minister of Australia. Later that day, Tony Abbott delivered his farewell speech, the carbon tax wasn't mentioned by name, simply 'I am proud of what we have achieved over the past two years ... Labor's bad taxes are gone'.[201]

Conclusion

Chapter 4 examined Australian climate policy and diplomacy during the Abbott Coalition Government, covering the period from September 2013 to September 2015.

In 2013 and 2014, we saw the Abbott Government and the Australian fossil fuel lobby agree that Australia's core national interest in responding to climate change was to reverse the apparent slide in Australia's industrial competitiveness after six years of Labor governments' climate policies (Rudd's ETS and Gillard's carbon price – 2007–2013). The Prime Minister was repeatedly explicit on this point, as was the MCA and the APPEA. To achieve this, the Abbott Government rolled out a domestic and international strategy to not only restore, but enhance, Australia's industrial competitiveness.

As we saw, the major change in Australian climate policy and diplomacy from September 2013 to September 2015 was the Abbott Government's abolishment of the Gillard Government's carbon price and the establishment of the Direct Action/ERF policy. This transition in domestic climate policy, and its international extension, can be understood as comprising two distinct phases designed to first *protect and restore*, then *advance and enhance*, the competitiveness of Australia's fossil fuel industry.

Phase one *protected* the competitive position of Australia's fossil fuel mining industry (reversing the slide). This phase's domestic dimension involved abolishing Gillard's carbon pricing legislation. As we saw, government and industry actors deployed the CTA and LL storylines to justify the abolition of the Clean Energy Act 2011. These storylines were initially (from September 2013 to June 2014) deployed to persuade Labor parliamentarians, particularly Labor Senators into passing the abolition bill; then later, in the new Senate (after July 2014), redeployed to pressure PUP

Senators to secure the same end. In this phase, in a series of Critical Discourse Moments – namely, Abbott's election victory in September 2013, the release of the Draft Exposure repeal bill in October 2013, and the introduction of the bill into the House of Representatives in November 2013 – which deployed the CTA storyline, the Abbott Government sought the entrench this storyline as the dominant frame from which to conceive carbon pricing in Australia (deeply subordinating the Rudd-Gillard era of the CNTA storyline dominating the framing of domestic carbon pricing). Above all else, in this period government and industry argued that the carbon price undermined industry competitiveness and abolishing it would help restore it. And on this basis, in July 2014, Australia abolished its price on carbon pollution.

Phase one's international dimension involved the following elements. First, removing climate change from the Prime Minister's agenda at regional and international events and gatherings, for example APEC, EAS, the G20 – and when pushed by journalists, use these events as a platform to deploy the CTA and LL storyline to pressure domestic senators into 'axing the tax'. Second, not attending UN climate events, including the Conference of the Parties to the UNFCCC, and similarly, when pushed use these events to argue for the removal for the domestic carbon price. Third, building alliances and coalitions of the willing with like-minded countries that also oppose carbon pricing (e.g. Canada under Stephen Harper). Combined: abolishing the domestic carbon price and erasing climate change from the international agenda – which included snubbing UN climate events, thus avoiding their obligations – would restore the competitiveness of the fossil fuel industry, argued government and industry.

Phase two *advanced* the competitive position of Australia's fossil fuel mining industry (a step up from protecting the industry). Domestically, as we saw, as the carbon price was in the final stages of being abolished, the Abbott Government commenced its Direct Action/ERF policy development process. The government and industry deployed the WW storyline to legitimise this policy. The ERF key design elements – crediting and purchasing of emissions, and its hugely flexible safeguard mechanism (among other things) – would serve to encourage foreign investment in Australia's fossil fuel sector. In this phase, two more Critical Discourse Moments deployed the CTA storyline, and on these occasions, to institutionalise this storyline as the dominant storyline to understand carbon pricing: first, the ERF policy development process (the Green Paper of December 2013 and White Paper of April 2014); and second, the ERF legislative process (commencing with the introduction of the ERF bill in the House of Representatives in June 2014). In October 2014, the ERF passed the Senate. Henceforth, the CTA storyline – and the notion that carbon pricing undermined the competitive position of Australia's fossil fuel industry – was the law of the land, obliterating the notion that delaying the implementation of a price on carbon would only serve to increase Australia's economic and environmental costs over time. Phase two's international dimension involved the following elements. First, Abbott sought to establish FTAs with Australia's largest coal and LNG customers – Japan, Korea, and China – which he achieved. Second, he toured Europe and North America encouraging companies to invest in Australia's fossil fuel resources. Third, in the aftermath of the abolition of the domestic carbon price, he used international events as a platform to deploy the LL storyline to justify abolishing the carbon price, as well as the WW storyline to legitimise the ERF – both were presented as reasons why foreign companies should invest in Australian industry (e.g. 'Australia is now open for business'). Fourth, he sought to build alliances with countries that were introducing Direct Action measures (e.g. Obama's Clean Power Plan) to help legitimise his domestic plan. Fifth, he established other (non-FTA) bilateral energy trading relations, for example, organising the sale of Australian uranium to India and encouraging India's investment in Australian coal.

Overall, Chapter 4 revealed the existence of a 'master discourse' about industrial competitiveness, shared between government and industry. This discursive structure both dominated the meaning of Australia's national interest on climate (and energy) policy, and shaped the field of decision making for government and industry actors in terms of what was deemed appropriate and inappropriate domestic climate policies and international diplomacy. This chapter also uncovered an 'ancillary discourse' about Liberal Party foreign policy traditions that directed and legitimated Abbott's alliance-focused climate diplomacy and his disregard for the UNFCCC's process. This discourse permitted Abbott to pursue an international climate and energy agenda that supported the 'master discourse' about competitiveness and those accompanying interests with relative domestic impunity compared to Gillard.

However, ultimately, Abbott pushed his competitiveness-based domestic and international climate/energy strategy too far. His relentless reminiscing about the abolition of the domestic carbon price combined with being repeatedly exposed as out-of-touch internationally (i.e. US–China deal at APEC; G20 Brisbane), contributed heavily to Party Room disquiet (particularly among party moderates), which ultimately led to his removal as Prime Minister by Malcolm Turnbull in September 2015.

Notes

1 Tony Abbott, 'Interview with Eddie McGuire, Mick Molloy and Luke Darcy', Triple M, Melbourne, 9 September 2013.
2 Tony Abbott, 'Interview with Karl Stefanovic and Lisa Wilkinson', Today, Channel 9, 10 September 2013.
3 Tony Abbott, 'Remarks at Swearing-In of First Abbott Government', Government House, Canberra, 18 September 2013. See also, Tony Abbott, 'Remarks at Joint Coalition Party Room Meeting', Parliament House, 13 September 2013.
4 Tony Abbott, 'A Team to Build A Stronger Australia', Media Release, 16 September 2013. See also, Tony Abbott, 'The Coalition will Restore Strong, Stable and Accountable Government', Media Release, 18 September 2013
5 'Abbott Shuts Down Climate Commission', The Age, 19 September 2013.
6 David Byers, 'New Industry Minister an Experienced Appointment', APPEA, Media Release, 16 September 2013.
7 Mitch Hooke, 'The New Coalition Government', Statement, 8 September 2013.
8 Mitch Hooke, 'The New Coalition Government', Statement, 8 September 2013. See also, Mitch Hooke, 'Australia's Carbon Tax: A Billion Dollar Deadweight on Mining', Statement, 19 September 2013.
9 Tony Abbott, 'Joint Press Conference', Parliament House, 15 October 2013.
10 Tony Abbott, 'Visit to Australia By New Zealand Prime Minister John Key', 2 October 2013.
11 See for example, Tony Abbott, 'Press Conference', Bali, Indonesia, 7 October 2013; Tony Abbott, 'Joint Press Conference', Canberra, 15 October 2013.
12 Tony Abbott, 'Press Conference', Brunei, 10 October 2013.
13 For example, Tony Abbott, 'Press Conference', Bali, Indonesia, 7 October 2013.
14 Tony Abbott, 'Joint Press Conference', Canberra, 15 October 2013.
15 'Repeal of the Carbon Tax Exposure Draft Legislation and Consultation Paper', Australian Government, October 2013.
16 Tony Abbott, 'Legislation to Repeal the Carbon Tax', Media Release, 15 October 2013.
17 Tony Abbott, 'Legislation to Repeal the Carbon Tax', Media Release, 15 October 2013.
18 Mitch Hooke, 'Mining Industry Pays Almost $117 Billion In Taxes and Royalties', MCA, Statement, 3 October 2013.
19 David Byers, 'Australia Needs Policy Clarity', APPEA, Media Release, 11 October 2013.
20 'New Report Confirms Gas is Australia's Natural Advantage', APPEA, Media Release, 8 October 2013.
21 Mitch Hooke, 'BREE Confirms Coal Industry's Ongoing Value to the Economy', MCA, Statement, 3 October 2013.
22 'New Report Confirms Gas is Australia's Natural Advantage', APPEA, Media Release, 8 October 2013.
23 Tony Abbott: 'Address to South Australian Liberal Party State Council', Adelaide, 19 October 2013; 'Address to Tasmanian Liberal Party State Council', Hobart, 26 October 2013.
24 Tony Abbott, 'Joint Press Conference', Canberra, 15 October 2013.

25 Tony Abbott, 'Doorstop Interview', Canberra, 14 October 2013.
26 See for example, Tony Abbott: 'Joint Press Conference', Canberra, 15 October 2013; 'Address to South Australian Liberal Party State Council', Adelaide, 19 October 2013; 'Address to Tasmanian Liberal Party State Council', Hobart, 26 October 2013.
27 See for example, 'Australia Makes a Bad Start at Warsaw Climate Change Meeting', The Conversation, 14 November 2013; 'Climate Change Talks: No Minister to Represent Australia', *The Guardian*, 7 November 2013; 'Australia Slides Down to Bottom on Climate Change Performance Index', *The Guardian*, 19 November 2013.
28 Tony Abbott, 'Press Conference', Parliament House, 12 November 2013.
29 Tony Abbott, 'Introduction of Clean Energy Legislation (Carbon Tax Repeal) Bill 2013', Speech, Parliament, 13 November 2013.
30 Tony Abbott, 'Interview with Leigh Sales', 7.30, ABC, 13 November 2013. See also, Tony Abbott, 'Interview with Lisa Wilkinson', Today, Channel 9, 13 November 2013.
31 'Industry Groups United: Carbon Tax Must Go', MCA, with Australian Chamber of Commerce and Industry, the Australian Industry Group, Business Council of Australia, Joint Media Release, 13 November 2013.
32 'Australia's Potential to Rival Qatar as The World's Largest Exporter of LNG at Risk', APPEA, Media Release, 13 November 2013.
33 Tony Abbott, 'House of Representatives Votes to Scrap the Carbon Tax', Media Release, 21 November 2013.
34 Tony Abbott, 'Prime Minister's Social Media Message', 24 November 2013.
35 Tony Abbott, 'Joint Remarks on Australia's Chairmanship of the G20', 25 November 2013.,
36 Tony Abbott, 'Australia Concludes FTA Negotiations with The Republic of Korea', Media Release, 5 December 2013.
37 Mitch Hooke, 'Minerals Council Welcomes Australia-Korea Free Trade Agreement', Statement, 5 December 2013.
38 'Minerals Council of Australia: Appointment of Chief Executive', MCA, Media Release, 3 December 2013.
39 'Emissions Reduction Fund, Green Paper', Commonwealth of Australia, 2013.
40 'Emissions Reduction Fund, Green Paper', Commonwealth of Australia, 2013, p. 4.
41 Greg Hunt, 'Emissions Reduction Fund, Green Paper', Commonwealth of Australia, 2013.
42 Tony Abbott, 'Press Conference', Davos, Switzerland, 21 January 2014.
43 Tony Abbott, 'Press Conference', Davos, Switzerland, 21 January 2014.
44 Tony Abbott, 'G20 Finance Ministers Meeting & Western Australian Senate Election', A Message from the Prime Minister, 23 February 2014. See also, Tony Abbott: 'Our Plan to Build a Strong Prosperous Economy', A Message from the Prime Minister, 9 February 2014; 'Joint Doorstop Interview with Dr Bill Glasson', Brisbane, 6 February 2014.
45 Tony Abbott, 'Address to the Australia-Canada Economic Leadership Forum', Melbourne, 24 February 2014.
46 'The Green Paper for the Emissions Reduction Fund', MCA, Submission, February 2014.
47 'The Green Paper for the Emissions Reduction Fund', MCA, Submission, February 2014.

48 'Emissions Reduction Fund Green Paper: December 2013', APPEA, Submission, lodged February 2014. See also, 'Good Design Crucial for Emissions Reduction Fund', APPEA, Media Release, 25 February 2014.
49 'Reducing Australia's Greenhouse Gas Emissions – Targets and Progress Review: Final Report', Commonwealth of Australia (Climate Change Authority), February 2014.
50 Greg Hunt, 'Climate Change Authority Report', Media Release, 27 February 2014.
51 Tony Abbott, 'Press Conference', Perth, 31 March 2014.
52 Tony Abbott, 'Joint Press Conference', Parliament House, 3 March 2014.
53 Tony Abbott, 'Address to the South Australian Liberal Party State Campaign Launch', Adelaide, 9 March 2014.
54 Tony Abbott, 'Remarks at the Western Australian Senate Election Campaign Launch', 11 March 2014. See also, Tony Abbott, 'Press Conference', Perth, 31 March 2014.
55 Tony Abbott, 'Doorstop Interview', Sydney, 10 March 2014
56 Tony Abbott, 'A Message from The Prime Minister – Cutting Red Tape', 16 March 2014.
57 Tony Abbott, 'Interview with Leon Byner', Radio FIVEaa, Adelaide, 13 March 2014.
58 Tony Abbott, 'Historic Free Trade Agreement Concluded with Japan', Media Release, 7 April 2014. See also Tony Abbott: 'Japan-Australia Summit Meeting', 7 April 2014; 'Joint Press Release with Prime Minister Abe', 7 April 2014; 'Joint Press Statement with Prime Minister Abe', 7 April 2014. Note: In July 2014, Prime Minister Abe visited Australia. The bilateral talks produced that same storylines and objectives. See, Tony Abbott, 'Joint Statement with Prime Minister Abe: Special Strategic Partnership for the 21st Century', 8 July 2014.
59 Brendan Pearson, 'MCA Welcomes Australia–Japan Free Trade Agreement', MCA, Statement, 7 April 2014.
60 Tony Abbott, 'Vision Statement for a Secure, Peaceful and Prosperous Future Between the Republic of Korea and Australia', Media Release, 8 April 2014.
61 Tony Abbott: 'Address to Australia Week in China Lunch', Shanghai, China, 11 April 2014; 'Address to Boao Forum for Asia', Shanghai, China, 10 April 2014.
62 'Emissions Reduction Fund, White Paper', Commonwealth of Australia, 2014.
63 Greg Hunt, Foreword, 'Emissions Reduction Fund, White Paper', Commonwealth of Australia, 2014, p. 2.
64 'Emissions Reduction Fund, White Paper', Commonwealth of Australia, 2014, p. 15.
65 Tony Abbott, 'Budget 2014', A Message from the Prime Minister, 10 May 2014.
66 Andrew Michelmore, 'Minerals Week – Chairman's Dinner Speech and Introduction to the Prime Minister', Canberra, 28 May 2014.
67 Andrew Michelmore, 'Minerals Week – Chairman's Dinner Speech and Introduction to the Prime Minister', Canberra, 28 May 2014.
68 Tony Abbott, 'Address to The Minerals Week 2014 – Annual Minerals Industry Parliamentary Dinner', Canberra, 28 May 2014.
69 Tony Abbott, 'Remarks at the French Business Leaders Reception', Australian Embassy, Paris, 5 June 2014. Tony Abbott, 'Press Conference', Paris, France, 6 June 2014.

70 Tony Abbott, 'Australian Business Delegation to Canada and The United States of America', Media Release, 3 June 2014.
71 Tony Abbott, 'Joint Press Conference with Prime Minister Stephen Harper', Ottawa, 9 June 2014.
72 Tony Abbott, 'Doorstop Interview', Ottawa, Canada, 8 June 2014.
73 Tony Abbott, 'Address to The American Australian Association Business Luncheon', New York, 10 June 2014.
74 Tony Abbott, 'Doorstop Interview', New York Stock Exchange, 10 June 2014.
75 Tony Abbott, 'Australian Business Delegation to Canada and The United States of America', Media Release, 3 June 2014. See also, Tony Abbott, 'Doorstop Interview', P-Tech, Brooklyn, 11 June 2014. Tony Abbott aligns Direct Action with Obama's Clean Power Plan see, Tony Abbott, 'Joint Doorstop Interview', Adelaide, 5 August 2015.
76 Tony Abbott, 'Joint Remarks with President Obama', The White House, 12 June 2014.
77 Tony Abbott, 'Doorstop Interview', P-Tech, Brooklyn, 11 June 2014.
78 Tony Abbott, 'Interview with David Speers', Sky News, 13 June 2014.
79 Tony Abbott, 'Houston Consulate-General', 13 June 2014.
80 Tony Abbott, 'Address to The Asia Society Texas Centre', Houston, 13 June 2014.
81 Greg Hunt, 'Carbon Farming Initiative Amendment Bill 2014', Speech, Australian Parliament, 18 June 2014.
82 Greg Hunt, 'Carbon Farming Initiative Amendment Bill 2014', Speech, Australian Parliament, 18 June 2014.
83 Tony Abbott, 'Delivering on Our Commitments', A Message from the Prime Minister, 22 June 2014.
84 Tony Abbott, 'Second Reading Speech – Clean Energy Legislation (Carbon Tax Repeal) Bill 2013', Parliament House, 23 June 2014.
85 Tony Abbott, 'Second Reading Speech – Clean Energy Legislation (Carbon Tax Repeal) Bill 2013', Parliament House, 23 June 2014.
86 'Al Gore Joins Clive Palmer to Back Emissions Trading Scheme for Australia', 7.30, ABC, 25 Jun 2014. See also, 'The Four Who Brought Together Clive Palmer and Al Gore', The Sydney Morning Herald, 27 June 2014.
87 Tony Abbott, 'Getting More Australians Into Work', A Message from the Prime Minister, 29 June 2014.
88 Tony Abbott, 'Interview with Chris Uhlmann', ABC AM, 1 July 2014.
89 Tony Abbott, 'Interview with Chris Smith', Radio 2GB, Sydney, 2 July 2014.
90 Tony Abbott, 'Joint Doorstop Interview', Melbourne, 3 July 2014.
91 Tony Abbott, 'Address to the Liberal National Party State Convention', Brisbane, 12 July 2014. See also, Tony Abbott: 'Boosting Jobs and Helping Families', A Message from the Prime Minister, 6 July 2014; 'Joint Doorstop Interview', Perth, 10 July 2014; 'Joint Press Conference', Sydney, 11 July 2014.
92 Tony Abbott, 'Government Delivers on Commitment to Abolish the Carbon Tax', 17 July 2014.
93 Brendan Pearson, 'Carbon Tax Repeal Will Promote Jobs and Investment Growth', MCA, Statement, 17 July 2014.
94 David Byers, 'Carbon Tax Repeal Removes Cost Burden on LNG Exporters', APPEA, Media Release, 17 July 2014.

95 Tony Abbott, 'Joint Statement with Prime Minister Modi', New Delhi, India, 5 September 2014.

96 For support of Adani see, Tony Abbott: 'Address to The Prime Minister's Business Delegation and Indian CEOs Lunch', Mumbai, 4 September 2014; 'Doorstop Interview', Mumbai, 4 September 2014. Also see, Tony Abbott: 'Joint Doorstop Interview', Canberra, 17 August 2015; 'Joint Doorstop Interview', Yass, 19 August 2015.

97 'UN Climate Change Summit in New York – As It Happened', *The Guardian*, 24 September 2014.

98 Tony Abbott, 'Interview with Fran Kelly', ABC Radio National, 16 September 2014.

99 Tony Abbott, 'Doorstop Interview', New York, 25 September 2014.

100 Tony Abbott, 'Address to The United Nations General Assembly', United Nations, New York, 25 September 2014.

101 Tony Abbott, 'Address to the Australian Food and Grocery Council Industry Leader's Forum', Parliament House, 1 October 2014.

102 Tony Abbott, 'Joint Doorstop Interview', Sydney, 8 October 2014

103 Tony Abbott, 'Joint Doorstop Interview', Moranbah, 13 October 2014.

104 Tony Abbott, 'Address to the Business Council of Australia Annual Dinner', Sydney, 28 October 2014.

105 Tony Abbott, 'Joint Press Conference', Melbourne, 31 October 2014.

106 'ERF Detail Crucial for International Competitiveness', APPEA, Media Release, 31 October 2014.

107 'Minerals Industry Priorities and Regularity Reforms', MCA, Booklet, 31 October 2019, p. 39.

108 Tony Makin, 'Australia's Competitiveness: Reversing the Slide', MCA, Report, September 2014. See also, Brendan Pearson, 'Australia's Competitiveness: Reversing the Slide', MCA, Statement, 3 September 2014.

109 'Senate Must Rethink One-Stop Shop in the National Interest', MCA, Media Release, 2 October 2014. Other members included APPEA, Business Council of Australia, National Farmers Federation, and Property Council of Australia. See also, Brendan Pearson, 'Reducing Project Delays Will Deliver $160 Billion Gain and 69,000 Jobs by 2025: New Report', Statement, 18 August 2014.

110 Tony Abbott, 'Joint Press Conference', Beijing, 10 November 2014.

111 'U.S.-China Joint Announcement on Climate Change', Beijing, China, 12 November 2014.

112 Tony Abbott, 'Doorstop Interview', Naypyidaw, Burma, 13 November 2014.

113 Tony Abbott: 'Doorstop Interview', Naypyidaw, Burma, 13 November 2014; 'Joint Press Conference', Canberra, 14 November 2014.

114 Tony Abbott: 'Doorstop Interview', Naypyidaw, Burma, 13 November 2014; 'The G20', A Message from the Prime Minister, 2 November 2014; 'G20 Summit', A Message from the Prime Minister, 9 November 2014.

115 Brendan Pearson, 'Coal Delivers a Clean Future for The Poor', Opinion, Australian Financial Review, 6 October 2014. See also, Brendan Pearson: 'Prime Minister Puts Coal's Future in Perspective', MCA, Statement, 4 November 2014; 'No Escape from Poverty Without Low Cost Energy', MCA, Statement, 7 November 2014.

116 'Natural Gas Can Deliver Economic Growth and Cut Emissions', APPEA, Media Release, 12 November 2014.

117 Brendan Pearson, 'Prime Minister Puts Coal's Future in Perspective', MCA, Statement, November 2014. 'Natural Gas Can Deliver Economic Growth and Cut Emissions', APPEA, Media Release, 12 November 2014.

118 The MCA: World Bank and IPCC officials, the International Energy Agency, the Manhattan Institute, ABARES, and Bill Gates. The APPEA: Deloitte Access Economic, the IPCC

119 Tony Abbott, 'Opening Remarks at First G20 Plenary Session', Brisbane, 15 November 2014.

120 Barack Obama, 'Remarks by President Obama at the University of Queensland', The White House, 15 November 2014.

121 Tony Abbott, 'Press Conference', Brisbane, 17 November 2014.

122 Tony Abbott, 'Joint Press Conference with Chancellor Merkel', Sydney, 17 November 2014.

123 Tony Abbott: 'Landmark China-Australia Free Trade Agreement', Media Release, 17 November 2014; 'Joint Press Statement with President Xi', Canberra, 17 November 2014.

124 Tony Abbott: 'Address to Parliament, House of Representatives', Canberra, 18 November 2014; 'Joint Press Statement with Prime Minister Modi', Canberra, 18 November 2014.

125 Tony Abbott, 'Joint Press Conference with President Hollande', Canberra, 19 November 2014. See also, Tony Abbott, '(final) Press Conference', Brisbane, 17 November 2014.

126 'G20 Leaders' Communiqué', Brisbane Summit, 15–16 November 2014.

127 Brendan Pearson, 'The Minerals Sector and The Australia-China Free Trade Agreement', MCA, Statement, 17 November 2014.

128 Brendan Pearson, 'The Minerals Sector and The Australia-China Free Trade Agreement', MCA, Statement, 17 November 2014.

129 'Minerals Exports: China Japan Korea', MCA Fact Sheet, November 2014.

130 Tony Abbott, 'Interview with Neil Mitchell', Radio 3AW, Melbourne, 5 December 2014.

131 Tony Abbott, 'Assisting the Global Response to Climate Change', Media Release, 10 December 2014.

132 Tony Abbott: 'Assisting the Global Response to Climate Change', Media Release, 10 December 2014; 'Joint Press Conference', Melbourne, 10 December 2014.

133 Tony Abbott, 'Assisting the Global Response to Climate Change', Media Release, 10 December 2014.

134 Tony Abbott: 'Interview with Karl Stefanovic', Today, Channel 9, 2 December 2014; 'A Message from the Prime Minister', 13 December 2014; 'Press Conference', Canberra, 21 December 2014; 'Interview with Lisa Wilkinson', Today, Channel 9, 22 December 2014.

135 Tony Abbott, 'Joint Press Conference', Colac, 30 January 2015.

136 Tony Abbott, 'Knights of The Order of Australia', Media Release, 26 January 2015.

137 Tony Abbott, 'Doorstop Interview', Canberra, 26 January 2015.

138 Tony Abbott, 'Interview with Neil Mitchell', Radio 3AW, Melbourne, 22 January 2015.

139 See for example Tony Abbott: 'Address to The National Press Club of Australia', Canberra, 2 February 2015; 'Interview with Paul Murray', Sky News, 5 February 2015; 'Interview with Ray Hadley', Radio 2GB, 4 February 2015

140 Tony Abbott, 'Joint Press Conference', Melbourne, 5 February 2015
141 Tony Abbott, 'Press Statement', Sydney, 6 February 2015.
142 Tony Abbott, 'Interview with Alan Jones', Radio 2GB, 6 February 2015.
143 Tony Abbott, 'Statement – Prime Minister's Office', Parliament House, 9 February 2015.
144 Tony Abbott, 'Joint Doorstop Interview', Murrumbateman, 11 February 2015.
145 Tony Abbott, 'Interview with Neil Mitchell', Radio 3AW, Melbourne, 12 February 2015. See also for discussion of carbon tax and pensioners, Tony Abbott, 'Interview with Ray Hadley', 2GB, 14 May 2014.
146 Tony Abbott, 'Joint Doorstop Interview', Sydney, 16 February 2015.
147 Tony Abbott, 'Interview with Patrick Condren', Radio 4BC, Brisbane, 18 February 2015.
148 Tony Abbott, 'Interview with Steve Austin', 612 ABC, Brisbane, 18 February 2015.
149 Tony Abbott, 'Joint Doorstop Interview', Adelaide, 20 February 2015.
150 Tony Abbott, 'Joint Doorstop Interview', Livingstone, Northern Territory, 21 February 2015.
151 Tony Abbott: 'Joint Press Conference with Prime Minister Key', Auckland, 28 February 2015; 'Joint Doorstop Interview', Rockhampton, 27 February 2015.
152 Tony Abbott, 'Doorstop Interview', Kalgoorlie, 10 March 2015. See also Tony Abbott, 'Interview with Kirstyn March', ABC Goldfields, 10 March 2015.
153 Tony Abbott, 'Joint Press Conference', Geelong, 31 March 2015.
154 Tony Abbott, 'Joint Doorstop Interview', Cressy, 30 March 2015.
155 Tony Abbott, 'Joint Doorstop Interview', Ringwood, 20 March 2015.
156 Tony Abbott, 'Joint Press Conference', Canberra, 18 March 2015.
157 Tony Abbott: 'Doorstop Interview', Sydney, 11 April 2015; 'Joint Press Conference', Canberra, 14 April 2015; 'Address to Australian Chamber of Commerce and Industry Luncheon', Sydney, 15 April 2015; 'Joint Doorstop Interview', Boronia, 16 April 2015.
158 Tony Abbott, 'Doorstop Interview', Sydney, 11 April 2015.
159 Tony Abbott, 'Address to Australian Chamber of Commerce and Industry Luncheon', Sydney, 15 April 2015.
160 Tony Abbott, 'Post-2020 Greenhouse Gas Emissions Reduction Target', 28 March 2015. See also Tony Abbott, 'Joint Press Conference', Hamilton Island, 21 March 2015.
161 'Submission on the Issues Paper for the Setting of Australia's Post-2020 Target for Greenhouse Gas Emissions', MCA, Submission, April 2015, p. 11.
162 'Setting Australia's Post-2020 Target for Greenhouse Gas Emissions: Issues Paper', APPEA, Submission, March 2015 (Lodged April 2015), p. 5.
163 'Submission on the Issues Paper for the Setting of Australia's Post-2020 Target for Greenhouse Gas Emissions', MCA, Submission, April 2015, pp. 1–3. For MCA advocacy on CCS and HELE in the latter part of 2015 see, for example, Greg Evans, 'New Publication: Delivering A Low Emissions Coal Future', MCA, Statement, 4 August 2015; Brendan Pearson, 'G7 Statement on Climate Change, Energy and Environment', MCA, Statement, 9 June 2015.
164 'Setting Australia's Post-2020 Target for Greenhouse Gas Emissions: Issues Paper', APPEA, Submission, March 2015 (Lodged April 2015).

165 'Submission on the Issues Paper for the Setting of Australia's Post-2020 Target for Greenhouse Gas Emissions', MCA, Submission, April 2015.

166 Paul Fennelly, 'Budget Recognises Significance of Oil and Gas Industry', APPEA, Statement, 12 May 2015.

167 Bruce Lake, 'Challenges and Opportunities in an Era of Change', APPEA, Speech, 18 May 2015.

168 Martin Ferguson, 'Closing Speech', APPEA, 20 May 2015.

169 Tony Abbott, 'Address to the Annual Minerals Industry Parliamentary Dinner', Parliament House, Canberra, 3 June 2015.

170 Tony Abbott, 'Address to the Annual Minerals Industry Parliamentary Dinner', Parliament House, Canberra, 3 June 2015.

171 Tony Abbott, 'Interview with Michael Brissenden', ABC AM, 13 May 2015. See also Tony Abbott: 'Interview with David Koch', Sunrise, Channel 7, 13 May 2015; 'Interview with Karl Stefanovic', Today, Channel 9, 13 May 2015; 'Interview with David Speers', AM Agenda, Sky News, 13 May 2015.

172 Tony Abbott: 'Joint Doorstop Interview', Adelaide, 21 May 2015; 'Joint Doorstop Interview', Ulverstone, 22 May 2015.

173 Tony Abbott, 'Joint Doorstop', Sydney, 5 June 2015. See also, Tony Abbott, 'Address to the 58th Federal Council of The Liberal Party of Australia', Melbourne, 27 June 2015.

174 Tony Abbott, 'Address to The Liberal National Party State Council', Brisbane, 11 July 2015.

175 Tony Abbott, 'Doorstop Interview', Parliament House, Canberra, 15 July 2015.

176 Tony Abbott, 'Joint Doorstop Interview', Sydney, 27 July 2015.

177 Tony Abbott, 'Doorstop Interview', Canberra, 15 July 2015.

178 Tony Abbott, 'Interview with Leigh Sales', 7.30, ABC, 23 July 2015.

179 Tony Abbott, 'A Message from the Prime Minister', 9 August 2015.

180 Tony Abbott, 'Joint Press Conference', Canberra, 11 August 2015. See also Tony Abbott, 'Australia's 2030 Emissions Reduction Target', Joint Media Release, 11 August 2015.

181 Tony Abbott, 'Joint Press Conference', Canberra, 11 August 2015.

182 Tony Abbott, 'Australia's 2030 Emissions Reduction Target', Joint Media Release, 11 August 2015.

183 'Australia's 2030 Emissions Reduction Target: Strong, Credible, Responsible', Commonwealth of Australia, August 2015.

184 Brendan Pearson, 'Australia's 2030 Emission Reduction Target', MCA, Statement, 11 August 2015.

185 'Annual Report, 2014–2015', APPEA, December 2015, p. 19.

186 'Emissions Safeguard Mechanism Rules Critical to Oil and Gas Industry's Competitiveness', APPEA, Media Release, 2 September 2015.

187 Tony Abbott, 'Address to the South Australian Liberal Party AGM', Adelaide, 15 August 2015. See also, Tony Abbott, 'Joint Doorstop Interview', Queanbeyan, 12 August 2015.

188 Previous iterations are not shown but were mostly present in this period i.e. $550 saving for households and families, pensioners benefiting, power prices declining, previous arguments about taxation, and attacks on Federal Labor and Bill Shorten.

189 Tony Abbott, 'Joint Doorstop Interview', Bamaga, 26 August 2015. See also, Tony Abbott: 'Joint Doorstop Interview', Henderson, 21 August 2015;

'Interview with Michael Brissenden', ABC AM, 28 August 2015; 'Joint Doorstop Interview with Colin Barnett', Perth, 13 September 2015; 'Joint Press Conference', 1 September 2015.

190 Tony Abbott, 'Joint Doorstop Interview', Wodonga, 4 September 2015.

191 Tony Abbott, 'Joint Doorstop Interview', Thursday Island, 25 August 2015.

192 Tony Abbott, 'Joint Doorstop Interview', Wodonga, 4 September 2015.

193 Tony Abbott, 'Interview with Leon Byner', Radio FIVEaa, Adelaide, 14 September 2015.

194 Tony Abbott, 'Address to Tasmanian State Council', Hobart 5 September 2015.

195 Tony Abbott, 'Address to the Nationals Federal Council', Canberra, 12 September 2015.

196 Tony Abbott, 'Joint Doorstop Interview', Port Bouvard, 22 August 2015.

197 Tony Abbott, 'Joint Doorstop Interview', Thursday Island, 25 August 2015.

198 Tony Abbott, 'Press Conference', Canberra, 6 September 2015.

199 Tony Abbott, 'Doorstop Interview', Port Moresby, Papua New Guinea, 10 September 2015. See also, Tony Abbott, 'A Strong and Prosperous Pacific', Media Release, 10 September 2015.

200 'Dutton Overheard Joking about Sea Level Rise in Pacific Islands', ABC News, 11 September 2015.

201 'Tony Abbott's Final Speech as Prime Minister of Australia', Sydney Morning Herald, 15 September 2015.

Conclusion
Government–industry compatibility?

This book was prompted by a puzzle: why have successive Australian governments of different political persuasions failed to adopt strong GHG mitigation reduction policies, despite Australia's high vulnerability to the physical impacts of climate change?

As we have seen, the orthodox response to this puzzle has highlighted the privileged access to government, and possible 'arm-twisting' tactics, of Australia's fossil fuel lobbies, which have a vested interest in preventing any significant action to reduce emissions. Guy Pearse's and Clive Hamilton's 'greenhouse mafia' hypothesis of 2006 and 2007 popularised this conspiratorial understanding. Rather than provide a comprehensive answer to this puzzle, this book has retained Pearse's and Hamilton's focus on government–industry relations but approached the relationship from a much broader understanding of power relations. Instead of looking for direct industry influence on government policy (which has already been demonstrated) this book asked: *what is the relationship between government and industry climate change policy discourse from June 2010 to September 2015?* This included an examination of both government and industry domestic economic discourses as well as government foreign policy discourses, which also provided an opportunity to track the two-level discursive game by the Gillard and Abbott Governments.

Chapter 2 laid out these key discourses. It showed that since the end of the Vietnam War, both Labor and Liberal governments have predominantly viewed Asia as a commercial opportunity rather than security threat, and accordingly, set forth a programme of structural reform to expand Australia's export orientated mining operations to fuel Asia's development, which, it was believed, would boost Australia's prosperity and also encourage social and political stability within the region. By 1991, two years after the end of the Cold War, both Labor and the Coalition believed that a primary role of the federal government was to institute competitive-based reforms that helped expand Australia's export orientated mining sector – competitiveness became a core national interest in that sense. This chapter also showed that since the end of the Second World War, Labor and the Coalition have disagreed about how best to secure Australia's economic and security interests – via multilateral forums and alliance-focused diplomacy respectively.

The book was able to show that the 'greenhouse mafia' explanation was limited and superficial when viewed against these pre-established economic and diplomatic discourses. In contrast, by situating the discourses of industry lobbyists within the broader historical context of the convergent and divergent economic and foreign policy discourses of Australia's two major political parties, and the reaction of federal governments' to war and peace in 1945, 1973, and 1989, this book was able to account for both continuity and change during the climate policy/diplomacy regression years from Gillard to Abbott.

Chapter 3 examined climate policy and diplomacy in the Gillard years, from June 2010 to June 2013, and Kevin Rudd's brief return to the Prime Ministership, from June 2013 to September 2013. It showed that key members of the Gillard Labor Government and representatives from the Australian fossil fuel industry (ACA, MCA, and APPEA) exhibited strong discursive compatibility about the importance of protecting the competitiveness of Australia's mining industry in climate policymaking. Gillard, as leader of a minority government, did focus on establishing a price on carbon pollution as the cornerstone of Australia's domestic response to climate change. But Labor nonetheless agreed with the fossil fuel industry that any carbon price (both the fixed price period and emissions trading system) must avoid raising the financial costs of mining in Australia compared to other countries that did not have a carbon price. However, Gillard had the added concern, perhaps as a result of the Greens Party's initial influence over Gillard's prospects of forming minority government and ongoing influence over the policymaking process, of ensuring that Australia's low pollution industry remained globally competitive as other economies began to pollute less. In short, the Clean Energy Act 2011 protected the competitiveness of Australia's existing fossil fuel sector (and the jobs and government revenue therein), but also incentivised Australia's future low pollution industries – in other words, Australia's future competitive position compared to other countries relied on keeping in lock-step with the global transition towards low pollution economies ('Australia cannot be left behind', as Gillard explained). So, we can see that Gillard's domestic climate policy sought to protect the competitive position of both existing and future industries, and critically for Gillard, present and future jobs (inter alia, existing and future interests).

The Gillard Government's diplomatic strategy on climate change – which prioritised climate multilateralism, particularly the UNFCCC processes – reflected these domestic considerations and interests: protecting existing Australian mining and future low pollution industries. Gillard, Greg Combet, and Kevin Rudd (as Minister for Foreign Affairs) strenuously argued internationally for a 'environmentally effective' agreement to be struck, which meant negotiating some form of GHG stabilisation deal between the big emitters, the US and China, which they believed could only be achieved if key 'building blocks' were in place, particular if REDD+ offsetting activities were included under the UNFCCC's CDM – permitting the importation of large amounts of cheap CERs into Australia's domestic scheme for liable industries to use to meet their obligations, and avoiding competitive disadvantages. The Gillard Government also made formal submissions to the UNFCCC stressing the importance of including REDD+ activities under the CDM in a future international agreement. So, Gillard's climate diplomacy was shaped, quite considerably, by the competitiveness discourse, however the Gillard Government's status as a minority government with the Greens Party and Labor's sense of obligation to respond to the call of climate multilateralism, based on its internationalist foreign policy identity, and the pull of international climate norms, strengthened the government's domestic and international responses to climate change. Kevin Rudd's brief return to the Prime Ministership broadly continued this domestic and international strategy, albeit favouring mining interests by bringing forward the ETS phase. In summation, in the Gillard years, climate policy and diplomacy protected the competitiveness of Australia's existing fossil fuel industries as well as incentivising Australia's future low pollution industries (keeping Australia competitive over time).

Chapter 4 examined climate policy and diplomacy in the Abbott years, from September 2013 to September 2015. It showed that the Abbott Government and the fossil fuel industry also exhibited strong discursive compatibility about protecting the competitiveness of Australia's mining industry in climate policymaking. Both the government and industry supported the abolition of Australia's price on carbon, the Clean Energy Act 2011, on the basis that it would restore competitiveness to the industry, and therefore, help encourage investment and secure jobs in the industry. Abbott's Emissions Reduction Fund, which replaced the Act, as Australia's centrepiece domestic climate policy offered $2.5 billion dollars of taxpayer's money to existing and prospective fossil fuel operations to encourage them to reduce their emissions. Given existing firms had already made changes to their production process to ensure they pollute less because of the carbon price, and new entrants into Australia's fossil fuel market would generally be lower emissions, the ERF can be understood as a climate policy that enhanced the competitive position of Australia's resources sector compared to competitor countries. In short, Abbott's domestic climate policy was designed to maximise the attractiveness of Australia's territory and resources, compared to competitor nations, to multinational fossil fuel mining companies.

Beyond the ERF, Abbott prioritised energy-based solutions to climate change such as developing CCS, gas/LNG and uranium exports. However, he rarely justified the development of these energies on the basis that they provided a solution to climate change (which even sets him apart from John Howard who did). Rather, they were framed as good for the economy, jobs, and growth independently of their lower GHG qualities. Industry lobbyists supported the solution that expanded the commercial operations of their corporate members. In all, however, government and industry promoted these 'solutions' to climate change because they protected their current and future investment in the sector, government tax revenue, and Australian jobs, among other things, such as dependent families and regional communities, as well as public hospitals and schools. The overriding concern was to avoid imposing any kind of competitive disadvantage on Australian industry compared to international competitors.

The Abbott Government protected and advanced Australia's mining interests in uranium, coal, and LNG by establishing alliance-focused relations, most notable, by finalising FTAs with Australia's three major coal and LNG consumers, Japan, South Korea, and China. Similarly to his justification for encouraging the expansion of the domestic energy-based mining industry, Abbott did not make a point of arguing that uranium deals or LNG exports would provide a lower GHG alternative (again, his conservative predecessor John Howard regularly did use this justification). Rather, Abbott advocated overseas that Australia was once again 'open for business' because he would, and later did, abolish Australia's price on carbon. In addition, he actively courted allies and fossil fuel companies in Europe, Canada, the US, and India to encourage them to invest in Australia's fossil fuel resources. Abbott avoided speaking about climate change at most international engagements, and repeatedly snubbed official UNFCCC negotiations and their lead-in events. Abbott's 'climate diplomacy' was driven by the competitive discourse, which understood the national interest as coterminous with the interest of the mining industry. This was compatible with the alliance-focused foreign policy tradition of the Liberal Party, which seeks to protect Australia's national interest by maintaining and establishing alliances and interest-based coalition, rather than working through the United Nations. In summation, in the Abbott years, climate policy and diplomacy also protected the competitiveness of Australia's existing fossil fuel industries (in a much more pronounced fashion than Gillard), but also incentivised international investment in Australia's fossil fuel resources.

The findings in this book can be explained in terms of the neo-Gramscian renovation of Putnam's two-level games model, which provides an expanded understanding of the domestic and international pressures visited upon the executive. That is, the 'win-set' size at the international level is not solely determined by the presence or absence of domestic veto players seeking to protect their pre-given interests (i.e. the greenhouse mafia). Rather, it is shaped by a confluence of domestic and foreign policy discourses that produce the meaning of the national interest and thereby determine the boundaries of legitimate policy and diplomacy.

Australia's regression years on climate policy and diplomacy from Gillard to Abbott continues to present day under the Morrison Coalition Government – which has simply toped-up the ERF with new funding allocation while Australia's GHG emissions have risen year on year since 2014. In the intervening years, several new climate policies, and policy designs, have been floated then abandoned. For example, the Turnbull Government's National Energy Guarantee debacle, which heavily contributed to Malcolm Turnbull being replaced as Prime Minister. This pattern of policy and political wreckage is likely to continue until such time as there is bipartisan support for a revisionist competitiveness discourse and a greater emphasis placed on cooperation. In a warmer world, cooperation will be key.

Index

Printed in the United States
by Baker & Taylor Publisher Services